W9-BCW-920

The Parents' Guide to
Baby-Led
Weaning

The Parents' Guide to
Baby-Led Weaning

Skip the purées and go straight to solids!

With
125
Recipes

Jennifer House, MSc, RD

Robert
ROSE

The Parents' Guide to Baby-Led Weaning
Text copyright © 2017 Jennifer House
Recipes copyright © 2017 Jennifer House and Robert Rose Inc. (see page 217)
Cover and text design copyright © 2017 Robert Rose Inc.

For complete cataloguing information, see page 220.

Disclaimer
This book is a general guide only and should never be a substitute for the skill, knowledge and experience of a qualified medical professional dealing with the facts, circumstances and symptoms of a particular case.

The nutritional, medical and health information presented in this book is based on the research, training and professional experience of the author, and is true and complete to the best of her knowledge. However, this book is intended only as an informative guide for those wishing to know more about baby-led weaning; it is not intended to replace or countermand the advice given by the reader's pediatrician. Because each baby and situation is unique, the author and the publisher urge the reader to check with a qualified health-care professional before pursuing any course of action where there is a question as to its appropriateness. The author and the publisher are not responsible for any adverse effects or consequences resulting from the use of the information in this book. It is the responsibility of the reader to consult a physician or other qualified health-care professional regarding his or her baby's personal care.

This book contains references to products that may not be available everywhere. The intent of the information provided is to be helpful; however, there is no guarantee of results associated with the information provided. Use of brand names is for educational purposes only and does not imply endorsement.

The recipes in this book have been carefully tested by our kitchen and our tasters. To the best of our knowledge, they are safe and nutritious for ordinary use and users. For those people with food or other allergies, or who have special food requirements or health issues, please read the suggested contents of each recipe carefully and determine whether or not they may create a problem for you. All recipes are used at the risk of the consumer. We cannot be responsible for any hazards, loss or damage that may occur as a result of any recipe use. For those with special needs, allergies, requirements or health problems, in the event of any doubt, please contact your medical adviser prior to the use of any recipe.

Design and production: Daniella Zanchetta/PageWave Graphics Inc.
Editors: Sue Sumeraj and Tina Anson Mine
Recipe editor: Jennifer MacKenzie
Proofreader: Kelly Jones
Indexer: Gillian Watts

Front cover image: Happy baby close-up © Dolgachov/iStock/Getty Images Plus
Back cover images: Baby boy eating © Kanmu/iStock/Getty Images Plus; Baby eating watermelon © Brave-carp/iStock/Getty Images Plus

The publisher gratefully acknowledges the financial support of our publishing program by the Government of Canada through the Canada Book Fund.

Canadä

Published by Robert Rose Inc.
120 Eglinton Avenue East, Suite 800, Toronto, Ontario, Canada M4P 1E2
Tel: (416) 322-6552 Fax: (416) 322-6936
www.robertrose.ca

Printed and bound in Canada

1 2 3 4 5 6 7 8 9 FP 25 24 23 22 21 20 19 18 17

Contents

Introduction

Welcome to this exciting time in your baby's life — starting solid food! Congratulations on making it through the first few months of your baby's life. Adding a baby to the family always means big changes, whether it's your first or fifth child. Now you're ready for another stage in your baby's life, with the introduction of solid foods.

Starting solids is a fun time for both you and your little one. Babies are often vibrating with anticipation to start eating real food just like Mom and Dad do. You'll enjoy watching as your baby explores new tastes and becomes a more official part of the family, with a space at the table. And this process of eating real food and joining family meals is accelerated if you choose to start solids using baby-led weaning.

It's a good idea to be educated about the benefits of baby-led weaning and how to practice it so you can make sure your baby gets all of the important nutrients she needs. This book will cover why you might want to use this method, when to start, what nutrients your baby needs, how to prevent choking, how to deal with allergies and what to feed vegetarian babies. Plus, it answers a ton of real-life questions parents often have when starting baby-led weaning, and offers sample meal plans and 125 recipes.

There's a lot to learn, so let's get started!

— *Jennifer House*

Benefits of Baby-Led Weaning

Some benefits of giving your baby full control with real food from the start include:

1. **Good nutrition.** Whole foods can be more nutritious than purées, which are often watered down.

2. **Less pickiness.** Early exposure to the different flavors and textures of family meals may help babies become more adaptable and decrease future picky eating.

3. **Faster dexterity development.** Your baby will build up chewing skills and finger dexterity sooner.

4. **A healthy relationship with food.** By not forcing your child to eat (no "Here comes the airplane!" with a loaded spoon), you allow him to listen to his appetite, which helps him build a healthy relationship with food.

5. **Healthy weight.** By giving your baby full control over what she chooses to eat — and how much — you'll help her grow into the weight that's naturally right for her.

6. **Ease and expense.** You don't have to make or buy puréed baby food. That makes life so much easier!

7. **Less stress for parents.** Baby-led weaning is easier on parents. Surveys show that parents of baby-led weaners are less worried about what their children eat and weigh, so they pressure and restrict food intake less often.

Part 1

Baby-Led Weaning Basics

What Is Baby-Led Weaning?

Did You Know?

An Age-Old Practice

Baby-led weaning is becoming more popular in developed countries, but it's not a new practice. It has been around for as long as babies have been born. In many countries around the world, it has always been the preferred way to start a baby on solids.

In North America, we use the term "weaning" to mean discontinuing breastfeeding. We won't be discussing weaning from the breast in detail in this book, but please continue to breastfeed for as long as you and your baby desire.

So what exactly is baby-led weaning? In this context, "weaning" means that your baby is starting to eat solid foods. You skip right past the stage at which you feed your baby puréed food from a spoon and allow him to feed himself real solid foods. Here are three key ideas that help to define baby-led weaning:

1. **Your baby self-feeds.** Rather than you spoon-feeding your baby, he is in charge of picking up the food and getting it into his own mouth. Your baby has full control, right from the start, over which foods he chooses to eat from what you've offered, and how much to eat.

2. **Your baby eats family food.** Quite quickly (even from the beginning, for some), you can offer your baby the same foods you are eating. There's no need to make extra "baby" meals. Ease is one of the major benefits of baby-led weaning.

3. **Your baby joins in family mealtimes.** Everybody sits together for meals, as your baby's schedule allows. You don't have to feed her purées and then sit down to your (now cold!) meal. Family mealtimes produce great benefits throughout your child's life and are a wonderful habit to start from the beginning.

My Story

I'm happy and honored to be your guide on your baby-led-weaning journey. I'm a registered dietitian and nutritionist from Canada. I have two degrees in nutrition (a BSc and an MSc) and am a member of the Dietitians of Canada and the College of Dietitians of Alberta. I operate a private nutrition practice called First Step Nutrition, specializing in young families. I speak to moms about starting solids and baby-led weaning on a weekly basis — it's one of my favorite topics! I am also a board member of the Calgary Breastfeeding Matters Group and a member of the local Attachment Parents' Village, positions that speak to some of my other passions.

Besides my professional work, I also have plenty of practical experience as the mom of three. When I first started my elder son, Nolan, on solids 9 years ago, recommendations were very different: "Start with purées and wait 3 days before introducing a new food." His first food was fortified infant cereal.

Four years later, I was ready to start solids with my daughter, Norah. I still had never heard of baby-led weaning. The first food I offered her was homemade puréed bison. She did *not* like that bison — or anything else I offered by spoon, for that matter. This didn't concern me, as it can be normal for babies to take a few weeks to become interested in solids. But shortly thereafter, my family was relaxing (as much as you can with two young kids!) on an all-inclusive Mexican vacation. I had brought along some pouches of baby purées and infant cereal, which I offered to Norah in the hotel room. They were still a no-go. Yet she would sit with the family at the dining table in the buffet, and you could tell that she was just dying to eat what we were eating. So I offered her a bun and a stick of fruit, and she was in heaven! Norah basically forced us to choose baby-led weaning (and she is still a stubborn child who knows what she wants). While I didn't choose this method for her, or know much about it at that point, I quickly learned how easy and enjoyable baby-led weaning is.

I'm sure many younger siblings are accidentally started on solids using baby-led weaning, either because they refuse to eat purées, as Norah did, or because their parents are far too busy to make and feed them puréed baby food. By the time my third child, Arden, was ready to start solids, I knew more about baby-led weaning and wanted to give it a try on purpose this time. While he did have the odd purée, Arden generally loved eating what the rest of the family was eating, and he enjoyed all foods. As a mom and dietitian who has practiced baby-led weaning with her own kids, I'm confident that I can teach you how to do it in a way that's both safe and nutritious for your baby.

Take a Relaxed Approach

You don't have to be militant about defining or practicing baby-led weaning. You may choose to offer your baby some puréed food along with finger foods. Or you may have already started with purées and are now looking to expand your baby's options. That's okay. You didn't damage or confuse your baby by offering him puréed baby food — despite what you read in that Facebook group or that online chat room, there is no evidence to support this idea.

Did You Know?

A Growing Movement

Baby-led weaning is trendy right now, but not a lot of health-care professionals are currently recommending it. However, this is slowly starting to change: the most recent recommendations from the United Kingdom and Canada identify soft finger foods as appropriate starter foods for 6-month-olds. As more research comes out on the benefits and safety of baby-led weaning, more health authorities and health professionals will likely start supporting it. I've recently seen many dietitians get on board — and I've trained some of them myself.

It's more important to be truly baby-led than to be an official "baby-led weaner." No matter how you start solids, don't force your baby to eat more or less than the amount he wants, or to eat certain sizes or textures of food before he can handle them.

What Are the Benefits of Baby-Led Weaning?

Baby-led weaning comes with many practical benefits. Many parents choose to use it because it's quick, enjoyable for your baby and inexpensive. If you work outside the home or have more than one child, you may especially value the ease and time savings. But there are some physiological reasons why baby-led weaning can be advantageous to your child, too. Here are seven ways in which baby-led weaning may benefit your little one — and your whole family.

Benefit #1: Good Nutrition

Store-bought baby food has definitely improved in taste and variety over the past few years. But one of the main ingredients is always water. This means that the calories and nutrition your baby receives are a bit diluted compared with what's contained in real table foods. Some parents worry that using baby-led weaning methods will lead to their babies consuming too little food and therefore too little nutrition. However, they don't consider that most puréed foods are mainly fruit and vegetable mixes that are naturally low in calories, fat and protein. Babies who are given regular table food have the potential to consume a wider variety of undiluted ingredients and therefore receive a more nutrient-dense diet.

Benefit #2: Less Pickiness

Baby-led weaning has the potential to decrease the risk of picky eating as your child gets older. While many babies are willing to accept or taste all foods, this often changes at around 18 months to 2 years of age. At this point, toddlers exert their growing independence by becoming more selective with food.

One research study found that a group of babies who were fed using baby-led weaning techniques had a slightly increased preference for all food categories except sweets when compared with a group of spoon-fed babies. While this preference has yet to be proven conclusively, there are a few theories about why toddlers and preschoolers who have been introduced to solids using baby-led weaning may be more adventurous with food. First, they were exposed to different textures and flavors early on, before the picky eating stage, when their taste buds are more malleable. Second, the flavors and combinations of real table foods are superior to those of most puréed baby food. Early and repeated exposure to foods in their whole, recognizable form may increase your baby's trust in those foods and willingness to eat them.

Baby-led weaning can also lead to decreased picky eating because the child is in full control of the amount he eats. There's no forcing him into an extra spoonful he doesn't want if he is feeding himself. Research has shown that the more a child is pressured to eat, the less he will actually consume.

Benefit #3: Dexterity Development

"Dexterity" is defined as "skill in performing tasks, especially with the hands." With baby-led weaning, your baby gets plenty of practice moving foods around with her hands, picking them up and getting them into her mouth. Research shows that dexterity doesn't develop based solely on your baby's age; it also depends on how much she practices the day-to-day tasks that require it.

The abilities to bite food, chew, move food around in the mouth and swallow also develop earlier than we once thought. By 6 months of age, most babies are capable of grasping food and making an early up-and-down munching motion, which allows their gums to mash soft solids. Again, the more your baby practices these skills during baby-led weaning, the earlier she will master them.

Benefit #4: A Healthy Relationship with Food

Did You Know?

Responsive Feeding

A caregiver practicing responsive feeding watches for, and listens to, the baby's hunger and fullness cues. Baby-led weaning gives babies full control to listen to these signals, so it is a highly responsive feeding method. Little ones can eat as much or as little as they choose without external influence.

Childhood obesity is becoming more common in developed countries, and baby-led weaning may be one way to help curb this trend. Children are born with the natural ability to eat until they are comfortably satisfied, then stop. However, if a baby is not fed responsively (see sidebar), he will lose his ability to listen to his hunger cues and eat for other reasons. One reason could be that Mom worries that her baby hasn't eaten enough and therefore tries to force another (unwanted) spoonful of food into his mouth. Another could be that Dad doesn't want to waste food and therefore plays airplane with the spoon to encourage his child to eat after he's stopped feeling hungry.

Other parenting habits can also contribute to children not listening to their appetites, which can lead to overeating. These can include forcing children to finish their dinner or to eat all of their vegetables. On the opposite end of the spectrum, parents of children who were born larger might feel obligated to limit their food intake. Unfortunately, this backfires and often encourages binge eating. Perhaps you were raised with some of these "food rules" and can see the negative impact it has had on your ability to listen to your appetite and your relationship with food.

By using the baby-led weaning technique — rather than these common tactics to get children to eat more or less than they want — your baby engages in responsive feeding and maintains full control over the amount of food he feeds himself. As he grows, he will continue to develop his ability to listen to his appetite, self-regulate his energy intake and build a healthy relationship with food. This is even more important than the nutrition he'll get — it is a gift that lasts a lifetime.

Benefit #5: Healthy Weight

Responsive feeding helps your child grow up with a healthy relationship with food and the ability to listen to her own appetite. One long-term outcome of allowing your baby to choose how much to eat is a decreased risk of obesity. Research is beginning to back up this connection (see Research Spotlight, opposite).

Food responsiveness, or the ability to eat according to appetite, is linked with healthier weights. So is longer duration of breastfeeding and later introduction to solid foods. Babies who lead the weaning process generally breastfeed longer than babies who are spoon-fed, and begin eating solids at a later age. These could be two more factors associated with baby-led weaning that could help your child grow into a naturally healthy weight.

There's another bonus, too: baby-led weaning can potentially be positive for the health and weight of your whole family. Once your baby is ready to start eating family foods, you may start to question your own diet. If you don't think your meals are nutritious enough for your little one, you might make some healthy changes to your menu.

Research Spotlight

Weight and Feeding Methods

A study conducted by Brown and Lee (2015) compared two groups of toddlers: one had started solids using baby-led weaning and the other had been spoon-fed. At birth and before starting solids, there was no significant difference between the weights of the two groups. After starting solids, only 8.1% of the baby-led weaners were over the 85th percentile for weight compared with 19.2% of the spoon-fed babies. The baby-led weaners were also more "satiety responsive," meaning they ate according to their appetite, and less "food responsive," meaning they ate just because the food was there, regardless of hunger.

In their study, Townsend and Pitchford (2012) examined 155 children aged 20 months to 6½ years. They also found that more spoon-fed babies were classified as overweight than baby-led weaners, independent of factors such as birth weight, parents' weights or socioeconomic status. These results suggest that baby-led weaning may lead to a child having a healthy body weight.

Benefit #6: Ease and Expense

Being a parent is hard: it's time-consuming and expensive. However, baby-led weaning can take away a bit of the burden. Sitting down with your baby and letting him feed himself whatever you're eating makes starting solids so much simpler. You won't have to spend time spoon-feeding your child. Plus, you won't need to spend lots of cash shopping in the baby-food aisle, or hours in your kitchen making and thawing homemade purées.

Baby-led weaning makes going out to restaurants easier, too. You don't have to cart along a baby plate, a spoon and pouches of purées. Just bring a bib, and have your baby feed himself pieces of appropriate food from your order. Whether it's a rib or a steamed carrot, most adult dishes have at least one component that a little one can eat happily.

Mom's Words of Wisdom

Noel loves baby-led weaning because "I am a working mom, so I don't have time to make my own baby food. Baby-led weaning saves me time. I was also interested in any steps I could take to decrease the chance that my child would be a picky eater."

Benefit #7: Less Stress for Parents

Parents who practice baby-led weaning have been found to be more relaxed and less stressed than parents who spoon-feed their children. One survey discovered that parents who used baby-led weaning felt that it was a healthy way to start solids, and that it was less anxiety-inducing and more convenient than traditional spoon-feeding. Turns out both babies and parents have a healthier relationship with food using this method!

Moms who choose baby-led weaning report feeling less stressed because they are able to eat at the same time as their babies. With spoon-feeding, it's easy to fall into the trap of taking the time to make baby food and feed your baby, but then forgetting to feed yourself. With baby-led weaning, you'll generally be making a single meal for the whole family, so you will be more likely to sit down and eat it. And since your little one can feed herself, you can enjoy her company and your meal at the same time.

Now you know what baby-led weaning is and the many benefits it offers parents and children. And while there are some potential risks, you'll learn how to work

Mom's Words of Wisdom

Jessyka was attracted to baby-led weaning because "I love the idea that Mom gets to have a hot cooked meal with her family, and that Baby gets to be involved in meal and family time."

through them in the next few chapters. So now that you're excited to start baby-led weaning — and, let's face it, your baby is keen to eat too — we'll cover how to identify the best time to start your baby down this path.

Research Spotlight

Lower-Pressure Eating

In a large study of 650 mothers in the United Kingdom, Brown and Lee (2011) found that parents who practiced baby-led weaning experienced less anxiety about starting solids. They also spent less time worrying about their babies' weight and how much their children were eating. In addition, they pressured and restricted their babies' food intake less often than parents who spoon-fed. Heaven knows there's enough anxiety surrounding parenting and all the choices you have to make. Why not make a simple feeding choice that will help reduce that stress?

When Is My Baby Ready to Start?

The World Health Organization, the American Academy of Pediatrics, Health Canada, the Australian Government Department of Health and the United Kingdom's National Health Service all currently recommend feeding babies breast milk exclusively until they reach 6 months of age. At 6 months, a baby's gut, immune system and kidneys are developed enough to introduce solids.

In 2002, the World Health Organization began recommending that babies begin solids at 6 months of age. Before that, the guideline was to introduce solids at between 4 and 6 months. But while the age at which to start solid foods has increased, the advice on *how* to do that hasn't changed in many countries — even though the skill and development of a 4-month-old is drastically different from that of a 6-month-old. However, the most recent recommendations from both Canada and the U.K. suggest that those first foods can include finger foods, which certainly seems like a step toward supporting baby-led weaning.

Mom's Words of Wisdom

Janelle says, "My pediatrician definitely pushed early introduction to baby food. I kept telling myself that breast milk had all the nutrition she needed." Courtney was also pressured into starting solids early but was firm in her decision to wait: "My nurse tried to push me into it, and I said no."

Starting Too Early: Debunking the Myths

Despite the current guidelines that recommend that babies wait to eat solid foods until 6 months of age, many are still introduced to them when they are 4 months old — or even younger. Here are four common (and inaccurate) myths that have parents believing their babies need solids before they reach the 6-month milestone.

Myth #1: My baby is big; he's hungry and needs "real" food.

Most babies younger than 6 months are not physically ready to start baby-led weaning. Therefore, you'll have to feed them puréed foods, many of which are less calorically dense than breast milk, especially if they are made with water. Monitor your baby's growth. If he is not gaining weight or is losing weight, then perhaps he might require solids before he reaches 6 months of age, if your pediatrician recommends it. However, just being "big" does not, in and of itself, mean a baby is ready for solid foods; his intestinal tract, immune system and dexterity are not necessarily better developed than those of a smaller baby.

Myth #2: My baby is small; she needs solid foods to help her gain weight.

First of all, there's nothing wrong with having a small baby. The 50th percentile on the growth chart is not a goal weight. It just means that, statistically, 50% of babies weigh more, and 50% weigh less. As long as your baby is growing consistently along her curve — whether that's the 1st, 50th or 98th percentile — then she is growing well. Again, if you start solids before she's 6 months old, you will be feeding her purées, many of which are less calorically dense than breast milk. Feeding her these extra foods may not help her gain weight even if she truly needs to.

> ### Did You Know?
>
> **Preemies May Need More Iron**
>
> If your baby was premature, she likely will need extra iron before she's 6 months old — but not necessarily from food. Talk to your doctor about iron supplements.

Myth #3: My baby will sleep better if I feed him solids.

I totally understand the torture that is sleep deprivation. I've experienced it myself, thanks to my babies, for most of the past 10 years! However, both research and parental experience have taught me that babies do not sleep better at night because they are eating solids. In fact, I've heard many moms say that their babies sleep *worse* after starting solids, often due to gas or constipation. There are many reasons why babies wake at night other than hunger, including teething, desire for comfort and just plain habit.

Most lactation consultants recommend continuing nighttime milk feeds until your baby is 12 months of age. You make more breast milk at night, and nursing can help both you and your little one get back to sleep quickly.

Myth #4: My baby is interested in food already.

Your baby is interested in everything you do, not just eating. At around 5 months, a baby will usually start exploring everything with her mouth. This is a great time to offer teething and mouthing toys, or even a plastic spoon to explore. While interest in food is one indicator that shows a baby's readiness to start solids, it's not enough of a reason on its own to start before the recommended age.

Starting Too Late: The Risks

Another trend, though less common than starting solids too early, is starting them later than recommended. Some moms aim to exclusively breastfeed until their babies are 9 or 12 months of age, even when they show signs of readiness for solids.

Breast milk *is* important; it is the main source of your baby's nutrition until he is a year old, and it can remain important beyond that, too. As the chair of a breastfeeding advocacy group, and having nursed each of my own children until age 3, I understand this fact very well. But as a dietitian, I also recognize the reasons why your baby needs some food other than breast milk, starting at around 6 months of age.

Did You Know?

Reflux Relief

Reflux — when stomach acids enter the esophagus and cause a burning feeling — is one reason why some doctors recommend starting solids before 6 months. Many babies receive some relief from this uncomfortable symptom after they begin eating table foods. If your baby has reflux, ask your doctor if you should begin solids early.

Did You Know?

Amazing Breast Milk!

Breast milk is the perfect first food for your baby. It contributes to a healthy gut and immune system, changes nutritionally according to your baby's age and even protects against viruses. However, at 6 months old, your baby is ready for more and needs some nutrients from solids to complement his milk intake.

Did You Know?

Not Just for Fun

You'll often hear the quote "Food before 1 is just for fun." But that's not 100% accurate. Your baby needs to be exposed to a variety of foods and textures starting at 6 months of age to avoid the potential risks associated with starting too late.

Health authorities recommend introducing solid foods around this time because there are specific risks associated with starting them too late. They are:

1. **Growth faltering.** In the second half of their first year, babies are still growing rapidly. Solid foods contribute calories that support rapid growth as your baby's appetite increases. Without them, normal growth is slowed.

2. **Micronutrient deficiencies.** It is especially important for babies to get iron from solid foods starting at about 6 months, because this mineral supports growth and brain function. While breast milk does contain easily absorbable iron, each liter offers only 0.35 milligrams, which isn't enough to meet your baby's needs starting at 6 months.

3. **Diminished motor skills and reduced acceptance of new foods.** The development of motor skills, such as chewing, can be delayed if your baby isn't exposed to finger foods before he's 9 months old. In addition, your child won't learn to accept different textures easily, making it more likely that you'll have a picky eater on your hands.

4. **Compromised allergy prevention.** Health experts recommend you introduce your little one to high-risk allergens starting at 6 months of age in order to promote tolerance. If these foods are delayed, your baby is at an increased risk of developing allergies.

Now, even though you've learned all of this, you can't *force* your baby to eat. If he is slow to accept solids, just continue to offer them regularly. Let your child play with his food and he will start eating it at some point. If you're worried about his iron status, you can always have your doctor give him a simple blood test to see if it's in the healthy range.

Signs of Readiness for Baby-Led Weaning

As you've learned, most countries currently recommend starting babies on solids at around 6 months of age. At this point in her life, your baby is developmentally ready and eager to move on to table food. But in addition to age, there are some other signs to watch for to ensure that your baby is ready to begin baby-led weaning.

- **Your baby has lost the extrusion reflex.** This is a reflex that babies are born with to help them suck and drink milk. The extrusion reflex causes anything that touches a baby's tongue to be automatically pushed back out, instead of kept in the mouth to move around and chew. This extrusion reflex is usually relaxed enough by 6 months to allow your baby to swallow solids, but it can be an issue if food is offered at a younger age. If your baby still displays the extrusion reflex when you start baby-led weaning at 6 months, it likely won't last for long. Just let her explore and continue to experiment with food.

- **Your baby can sit up well in his high chair.** Your baby needs to have solid head and neck control, as well as good arm and trunk strength before starting solids. Why? Two reasons: first, he needs to be able to lean forward to spit food out (to prevent choking) and, second, he must be able to reach for food and bring it to his mouth independently.

  There is some debate about whether babies need to be able to sit with support or sit on their own before starting baby-led weaning. Most instructors who teach this feeding method encourage you to start only once your baby can sit on his own without assistance. Personally, my two boys were late independent sitters (they were between 8 and 9 months old), but they still successfully managed solids earlier than that. I wouldn't have felt comfortable waiting until they were older, knowing that they needed the nutrition from table foods starting at 6 months.

  However, personal anecdotes aren't scientific evidence, so I spoke with an occupational therapist who specializes in feeding babies to see what she thought about this issue. She agreed that it is fine to start solids before your child can sit on his own, but only as long as your baby can sit well *with support*. This means that he can sit up in his high chair without leaning backwards and, without using his hands to support and balance himself, can reach for food and bring it to his mouth.

Did You Know?

Adjusted Age

For premature babies, use their adjusted age to determine when to begin baby-led weaning. This means you will be offering solids 6 months after their due date, not their birth date. Before this time, make sure to talk to your doctor about iron supplementation, as preemies may need a little boost in this area.

Did You Know?

Buy Smart

Some high chairs are built with a slightly reclined seat. This is unsafe, because it puts your baby in a position where food can more easily fall to the back of his throat and cause choking. Make sure to buy a high chair that doesn't allow him to lean back.

- **Your baby can pick up foods using her palm.** One common myth is that your baby needs to have a pincer grasp before starting self-feeding. A pincer grasp is the ability to pick up small pieces of food between the thumb and forefinger. However, at age 6 months, a palmer grasp works just fine. Your baby will be able to pick up large pieces of food with her palm and make a fist, bring them to her mouth and munch on whatever she grabs. She will develop a pincer grasp with practice, likely between 8 and 10 months.

- **Your baby seems excited to eat and grabs at your food.** I remember my babies just vibrating with anticipation to eat food at about 5½ months of age. While little ones are interested in *everything* you do, a baby that is almost ready to start enjoying family food may seem especially fascinated by the contents of your plate and try to snatch it.

What If My Baby Isn't Ready for Baby-Led Weaning at 6 Months?

While baby-led weaning will work for the majority of babies, not *all* babies are ready to start solids using this method (see Research Spotlight, opposite). Premature babies are one group in particular that can sometimes have a harder time managing solid foods and unfamiliar textures. But using the baby's corrected, or adjusted, age — that is, counting his age from his due date rather than his birth date — will help ensure your preemie is developmentally ready to start self-feeding. Premature babies also have higher requirements for iron, because they don't get the benefits of that full third trimester in their mom's womb to build up their stores of this important mineral. Your doctor may recommend an iron supplement.

Babies need to be able to get food to their mouths, chew and swallow safely before they can practice baby-led weaning. That means children who develop a bit more slowly — and their parents — may find self-feeding extra-challenging from the start. If your little one isn't reaching out and putting objects in his mouth (as in, everything he can get his hands on!), then you may have to reconsider how you approach baby-led weaning.

You can definitely still offer your baby finger foods around 6 months of age; even if he isn't able to handle them and feed himself, the practice will help improve his skills. In the meantime, it's still important that your baby gets nutrients from solids. There is no evidence that feeding your child purées will harm him, so I encourage you to be truly *baby-led*, and give your baby what he needs, just in a different form.

Research Spotlight

Exceptions to the Rule

A study by Wright et al (2011) analyzed feeding and developmental data from 510 babies at the ages of 6 weeks, 4 months and 8 months. Parents were asked if their babies had started solids yet, when their babies had reached out for foods, when their babies were given their first finger foods, and how often they were eating finger foods. The authors confirmed that most 6-month-old babies have the motor skills, physical stamina and interest in eating required to start baby-led weaning. In the 8-month study questionnaire, it was reported that 56% of the babies had first reached out for food before 6 months, but 6% were still not reaching out for food at 8 months of age. The authors concluded that baby-led weaning is feasible for most babies, but the small percentage that are not reaching out for solids may need initial spoon-feeding.

How to Prep for Baby-Led Weaning Before 6 Months

Did You Know?

Hard Munchables

These practice foods include raw jicama, celery, Parmesan rind, rib bone and carrot. If you're not comfortable offering food items as hard munchables, you could also offer plastic baby spoons to chew on. Make sure the item is long enough for your baby to grasp and that it reaches into the back of her mouth. It must also be hard enough that she can't bite off a chunk with her gums.

There's plenty you can do before your baby is ready for solids to help her prepare. Start by wearing her on your back in a carrier when you're cooking dinner, then let her sit in your lap while you eat. This allows your little one to start experiencing some of the exciting smells of family food.

At around 5 months of age, your baby will start putting everything she can get ahold of into her mouth. This is called mouthing, and it's actually a great way for her to learn. Mouthing will help her figure out how to move her tongue, lips and jaw in different ways than the sucking motion she's used to. It also helps develop the muscles of her mouth to increase strength and coordination, decrease the extrusion reflex (see page 19) and practice a munching-chewing movement pattern. Providing long stick-shaped toys that your baby can mouth will help decrease her gag reflex so that it's not as sensitive when she starts eating. If your child isn't starting to mouth on her own by 5 months, you can assist her by putting her hand on a mouthing toy, placing your hand over hers and guiding it to her mouth.

Once your baby is ready to sit in a high chair with support, bring her to the table for family meals in her new seat. Hand her a hard munchable (see sidebar) to mouth while you eat. This way, she feels like she is part of the family activity and can practice her skills. If your baby doesn't have teeth yet, she will not be able to bite off a piece of that hard munchable, chew and swallow it, but she will be able to experience its texture and possibly some of its flavor. This repetition will help further diminish your little one's sensitive gag reflex, which will be an asset when it comes time to actually eat.

Now you have an idea of when your baby will be ready to start baby-led weaning and what you can do to prepare. Coming up next, we will talk nutrition, and which are the most important nutrients your baby needs from food.

Important Nutrients for Your Baby

A popular but inaccurate saying that people repeat, especially in the baby-led weaning community, is "Food before 1 is just for fun." It's true that the first few months of your baby's experience with solid food will include a lot of learning through play, and trying out different tastes and textures — which can result in him eating not very much. Plus, some babies are more eager to consume food than others, and you certainly can't (and don't want to) force or pressure your baby to eat.

However, there are some crucial nutrients that your baby needs to start getting from food at around 6 months of age. On top of extra energy through calories, your baby especially needs iron. One of the risks of baby-led weaning is low iron intake, as parents often don't offer iron-rich finger foods and don't serve iron-fortified infant cereal. But with a little planning, you can avoid this issue. Let's take a look at why getting enough calories and certain nutrients is so important, and some food sources that work well for baby-led weaning.

> **The first few months of your baby's experience with solid food will include a lot of learning through play, and trying out different tastes and textures.**

Why Is Iron So Important?

Babies and children need iron for their brains and bodies to develop normally, and for their immune systems to work well. Iron helps the body make hemoglobin, which carries oxygen through the blood to all cells of the body. Hemoglobin is what gives color to red blood cells. When you don't have enough iron, red blood cells become small and pale, and a condition called anemia develops. When you're anemic, your red blood cells can't carry enough oxygen to your body's organs and muscles. Anemia in babies and children can lead to neurological problems, such as poor attention span, trouble concentrating and social withdrawal, which can last for decades — even after the anemia is resolved.

Your newborn baby has enough iron to support her growth for the first few months. This storehouse is built up during her time in your womb. The iron level your baby is born with depends on three factors:

1. **Mom's blood iron levels in pregnancy.** If you had low iron levels when you were pregnant, your newborn is more likely to have smaller iron stores.

2. **The length of the pregnancy.** Most of your baby's iron stores are built up in the last trimester of pregnancy. Premature babies don't benefit from this time to amass a full supply of iron, so many of them require iron supplements.

3. **How the umbilical cord was clamped.** A study conducted by Andersson et al (2011) reported that if a mother chose delayed cord clamping (see sidebar) after her baby's birth, her newborn had higher iron stores.

Recommended Intakes of Iron

Your baby needs to consume very little iron (about 0.27 milligrams per day) until he reaches about 6 months of age, thanks to the iron stores built up in his blood before birth. Between 7 and 12 months of age, his requirement jumps all the way up to 11 milligrams of iron per day — more than an adult male needs! This number is the recommended daily allowance (RDA) value set by the United States and Canada, which is the "level sufficient to meet the nutrient requirements of 97% to 98% of healthy people within each age group." This number takes into account the small amount of iron people typically absorb from plant-based foods, and compensates for a low intake of vitamin C, which helps increase iron absorption. So while 11 milligrams per day seems very difficult to achieve, if you are offering your baby meat and vitamin C–rich foods, he will absorb iron at a higher rate than is assumed by the scientists who set this RDA value.

What about iron from breast milk? Your baby's main source of nutrition in the first year is still milk. Breast milk is the perfect first food for your baby, supplying everything he needs to grow and be healthy for the first 6 months of life. It is still the mainstay of your baby's diet for the remaining months of that first year, and continues to be important for as long as you breastfeed.

However, breast milk is low in iron, even though it's easily absorbable. For example, your 8-month-old may consume about 4 cups (1 L) of milk per day, which provides only about 0.4 milligrams of iron. And while that may seem odd, this low iron level might actually be helpful. One theory is that bacteria and viruses thrive in an iron-rich environment, so perhaps taking in less of this mineral protects your baby during his most vulnerable first 6 months of life. But once your baby's iron stores from before birth run out at around 6 months, it is important to add iron into his diet to supplement breast milk and support growth.

Recommended Iron Intake

Age	Recommended Daily Allowance
0–6 months	0.27 mg per day*
7–12 months	11 mg per day
1–3 years	7 mg per day

* This value is classified as an adequate intake (AI) instead of a recommended daily allowance (RDA). AIs are based on the approximate intake of the nutrient by that group, so exclusively breastfed babies from ages 0 to 6 months take in about 0.27 mg of iron per day.

Source: Institute of Medicine, 2001.

Signs of Low Iron in Babies

If your baby was a preemie or you had low iron stores during pregnancy, you want to be especially on guard for these symptoms. There are a number of signs of iron deficiency you can watch for:

- Slow weight gain
- Little or no appetite (which creates a cycle that further contributes to slow weight gain)
- Decreased physically activity
- Paleness
- Fatigue
- Frequent illness

If your baby shows some of these signs, take her to the doctor and request a blood test to check her iron level. While moms often worry about having a doctor or nurse draw blood, many times the baby doesn't even notice it's happening! The American Academy of Pediatrics actually recommends that all 12-month-olds have a blood test to check their iron levels. If the test reports a low level, you can give her an iron supplement, which will help prevent anemia.

Research Spotlight

Iron Deficiency and Anemia

Iron deficiency is certainly not uncommon, but the prevalence of iron deficiency and anemia varies according to the population studied. One Canadian study (Zlotkin et al, 1996) looked at middle-class infants ranging from 8 to 15 months of age in four different cities and found that an average of 33.9% had iron deficiency and 4.3% had anemia.

Food Sources of Iron

There are two types of iron present in food. Understanding the difference between them will help you feed your little one plenty of this vital mineral.

Heme iron, found in meat and fish, is the more absorbable form; people absorb it at an average rate of 15%. Some food sources of heme iron include bison, beef, liver, clams, sardines, chicken and turkey.

If you're feeding your baby heme iron–rich meat during baby-led weaning, cook it until it's very tender and easy to eat. Ground meat in sauce, meatloaf and meatballs are easier for little ones to consume than steak. Your baby *can* get small amounts of iron from sucking on a large hunk of steak (which might be a popular choice!), but he won't get nearly as much as he would from actually chewing and swallowing the meat itself. Another idea is to cook a tender pork or beef roast in the slow cooker or pressure cooker to shred for your little one. These appliances also create tender ribs and chicken thighs, which are easy for your baby to grasp and chew on.

Did You Know?

Try Something Different

Dark chicken and turkey meat contains more iron than white breast meat. And don't assume that your baby won't like sardines and clams just because you don't — you'd be surprised at what babies will enjoy.

Non-heme iron, found mostly in plant-based foods, is the less absorbable form; people absorb it at an average rate of 5%. Some food sources of non-heme iron include legumes and beans, such as chickpeas and lentils; egg yolks; fortified infant cereal; blackstrap molasses; wheat germ; tofu; and dried fruit, such as raisins and apricots.

There are lots of ways to offer non-heme iron sources during baby-led weaning. Try frying an egg and slicing it into strips. Once your baby develops a pincer grasp, you can give him scrambled eggs and some black or other beans. Try removing the skins from chickpeas and splitting them in half, or making them into hummus. You can also serve vegetarian chili with beans. To make kidney beans a safer size to eat and prevent choking, squish them between your fingers before serving.

Blackstrap molasses is also high in non-heme iron, so add it to your baking when you can, along with some wheat germ. Or coat banana or avocado pieces with a little wheat germ or dry iron-fortified infant cereal. Firm tofu is another source; try grating it for use in recipes, slicing it into thin strips for munching or stir-fries, or blending it in smoothies. Chop dried fruits, such as apricots, prunes or raisins, and offer them as-is, or add them to muffins or hot cereal so they soften and are easier to eat.

Winning Combinations

Consuming an iron source with a vitamin C source boosts iron absorption. Vitamin C is an especially good partner to sources of non-heme iron, which are not naturally well absorbed. Vitamin C is found in fruits and veggies, such as citrus, berries, broccoli and bell peppers. Luckily, sources of iron are often naturally delicious paired with sources of vitamin C. Try some of these nutritious combinations to start.

Dish	Iron Source(s)	Vitamin C source(s)
Pasta with meat sauce	Enriched pasta and beef	Tomatoes
Tofu stir-fry	Tofu	Bell peppers and broccoli
Fruit and veggie smoothie	Spinach and hemp hearts	Mango
Cereal with fruit	Fortified cereal	Berries

5 Ways Baby-Led Weaners Can Get Enough Iron

A vitamin C–containing fruit or veggie served as part of a meal will increase iron absorption.

1. **Offer a source of iron at each meal.** This could include eggs, chicken thighs or drumsticks, meatloaf, shredded beef or pork roast cooked in the slow cooker or pressure cooker, or black beans. Some excellent recipes to try: Beginner Eggs (page 100), Peanut Butter Cereal Fingers (page 104), Lentil Patties (page 108), Burgers for Beginners (page 111) and Starter Pork Ribs (page 113).

2. **Include a source of vitamin C at each meal.** A vitamin C–containing fruit or veggie served as part of a meal will increase iron absorption. For example, top iron-fortified pancakes with fruit compote, serve lentils with stewed tomatoes, or add tofu to a fruit smoothie.

3. **Add some iron-fortified infant cereal.** One creative way to boost your baby's iron intake is to add this to finger food recipes, such as Fluffy Iron-Rich Pancakes (page 102) or Avocado Muffins (page 107). Once your baby has developed a pincer grasp, you can offer finger-friendly fortified cereal from the toddler aisle, soaked in milk.

4. **Make snacks count.** These mini-meals are another opportunity to include iron-rich foods. Try puréed meat as a spread or dip with toast or crackers. It's like pâté for babies!

5. **Cook with cast-iron.** Cast-iron pots safely add extra iron to the dishes cooked in them. If you don't have one, you can add a product called Lucky Iron Fish to your regular pots and pans and achieve the same result. See the Resources (page 220) for where to find these gadgets.

Food Sources of Iron

Here are some common iron-containing foods that are delicious choices for your baby. Each serving may offer only a small amount of this mineral, but they do add up over the course of the day. If you're eyeballing baby-sized portions, 1 ounce (30 grams) is about the same size as one-third of a deck of cards, or one-third the size of your palm.

Food	Serving size	Iron
Clams, canned, drained	1 oz (30 g)	8.0 mg*
Iron-fortified infant cereal, prepared	¼ cup (60 mL)	3.7 mg
Tofu, cubed	¼ cup (60 mL)	3.3 mg
Soybeans (edamame), shelled, cooked	¼ cup (60 mL)	2.2 mg
Beef liver, cooked	1 oz (30 g)	1.9 mg*
Dried apricots	¼ cup (60 mL)	1.9 mg
Iron-fortified toddler cereal (finger food)	¼ cup (60 mL)	1.8 mg
Lentils, cooked	¼ cup (60 mL)	1.7 mg
Spinach, cooked	¼ cup (60 mL)	1.7 mg
Hemp hearts	1 tbsp (15 mL)	1.4 mg
Chickpeas, cooked	¼ cup (60 mL)	1.2 mg
Prunes	¼ cup (60 mL)	1.2 mg
Bison, cooked	1 oz (30 g)	1.1 mg*
Kidney beans, cooked	¼ cup (60 mL)	1.0 mg
Shrimp, cooked	1 oz (30 g)	0.9 mg*
Beef, cooked	1 oz (30 g)	0.8 mg*
Sardines	1 oz (30 g)	0.8 mg*
Raisins	¼ cup (60 mL)	0.8 mg
Turkey, dark meat	1 oz (30 g)	0.7 mg*
Wheat germ	1 tbsp (15 mL)	0.7 mg
Egg, whole, cooked	1 large	0.7 mg
Lamb, cooked	1 oz (30 g)	0.6 mg*
Quinoa, cooked	¼ cup (60 mL)	0.6 mg
Pasta, enriched, cooked	¼ cup (60 mL)	0.5 mg
Tuna, light, canned in water, drained	1 oz (30 g)	0.4 mg*
Oatmeal, instant, cooked	¼ cup (60 mL)	0.4 mg
Chicken breast, cooked	1 oz (30 g)	0.3 mg*
Pork, cooked	1 oz (30 g)	0.3 mg*
Salmon, cooked	1 oz (30 g)	0.3 mg*

* A source of heme iron, which is absorbed two to three times better than non-heme iron.

Getting Enough Calories and Fat

> **It is important that your child gets enough iron and calories from food starting at around 6 months to supplement her breast milk intake.**

Baby-led weaning can sometimes pose another risk: your little one might not get enough calories. This could become a concern if your baby is not ready for baby-led weaning at the typical 6 months of age. Most babies *are* ready to feed themselves at that point, but some are not (see pages 20–21). Those that were born prematurely, have developmental delays or are just taking a bit longer to build the strength and dexterity needed to feed themselves can fall into this category.

It is important that your child gets enough iron and calories from food starting at around 6 months to supplement her breast milk intake. Therefore, I encourage you to be *truly* "baby led." If she is not able to feed herself at 6 months, continue to offer finger foods but consider supplementing her diet with some puréed foods. While I do believe in the benefits of baby-led weaning, it's most important that your baby gets adequate nutrition — and there is no harm in feeding a mixed diet of both purées and finger foods. Despite what you might read online, your baby will not be damaged or get confused.

For most of you who do have babies that can feed themselves and start baby-led weaning right on time, should you still be concerned that your baby may not get enough calories? Yes, but only if you offer an unbalanced diet. Multiple surveys and studies show that most parents offer fruits or veggies as starter foods. So what's wrong with introducing just fruits and vegetables? They are certainly healthy foods, full of vitamins and minerals, and should make up part of your baby's diet; however, they don't contain enough calories (or iron) to make up *all* of your baby's diet.

So how do you make sure you offer plenty of high-calorie foods to your baby? Serve all of the food groups from the start, including meat and alternatives, dairy products and grains — not just fruits and vegetables. Fat is the macronutrient that contains the most calories per gram, so offering higher-fat foods will ensure that your baby consumes high-calorie foods. Babies need a higher-fat diet than adults anyway, for growth and brain development. Much of your baby's fat intake will come from breast milk, but it's still wise to offer high-fat food choices at every meal. For example, spread butter, peanut butter or mashed avocado on toast fingers instead of serving them plain. Some other tasty high-fat food choices are full-fat cheese, full-fat plain yogurt, nut butters, meat, coconut oil, hemp hearts and eggs.

Vitamin D

It is important that your baby gets 10 micrograms, or 400 international units, of vitamin D per day. This micro-nutrient works along with calcium to strengthen bones, and may play a part in the prevention of certain cancers, as well as autoimmune disorders, such as diabetes and multiple sclerosis.

There are a few foods that are good sources of vitamin D, including fatty fish. And our bodies produce vitamin D when skin is exposed to sunlight. However, dark-skinned babies, those who live in northern countries or regions (such as Canada or Alaska) and those who are always covered with clothing and sunscreen (as recommended by dermatologists) are at higher risk of vitamin D deficiency. This is why experts recommend that you give your baby vitamin D drops daily from birth on — even a few drops every few days is fine if you find them hard to remember in the sleep-deprived brain fog of early parenthood.

> Experts recommend that you give your baby vitamin D drops daily from birth on — even a few drops every few days is fine if you find them hard to remember in the sleep-deprived brain fog of early parenthood.

Omega-3 Fats

For a child under 1 year of age, the adequate intake (AI) value for omega-3 polyunsaturated fats is 0.5 grams (500 mg) per day. Omega-3s are essential fats, meaning our bodies can't make them, so we need to get them through food or supplements.

A specific type of omega-3 called docosahexaenoic acid (DHA), found in algae and fish, is especially important for your baby's brain, eye and nervous system development.

Did You Know?

Safe Seafood Choices

Good low-mercury fish choices that contain omega-3 fats include salmon, shrimp, tilapia, cod, trout, haddock, halibut, bass, sole and canned light (not white) tuna. For more information, visit the Environmental Working Group's mercury info site at www.ewg. org/research/ewg-s-consumer-guide-seafood/mercury-toxicity.

Behavior, learning and focus may be improved if your baby gets adequate omega-3s throughout your pregnancy and in the first 2 years of life. New research suggests that these fats may also help prevent asthma and preterm labor (Bisgaard et al, 2016; Olsen et al, 2000). As a nursing mom, you can pass DHA through your breast milk to your baby, so it's important that you eat fatty fish, such as salmon, twice a week or take a fish oil supplement daily. Once you start your baby on solids, you can also offer him low-mercury fish (see sidebar) multiple times per week. Note that while walnuts, flax seeds and canola oil do contain omega-3 fat, it's a different form that's not as useful to your baby as DHA.

Making Baby-Led Weaning Work Nutritionally

It's understandable to ask yourself this question: Since it's so important for my baby to get enough calories and nutrients from foods, can a baby-led weaning program cover those needs? The answer is yes — if you do a little homework.

One study by Morison et al (2016), compared the nutrient intakes of 6- to 8-month-old baby-led weaning babies with those of traditional spoon-fed weaners. Participants filled out a feeding questionnaire and a weighed diet record (weight of food offered and weight of food left over). The authors found that the baby-led weaning group had higher average intakes of total fat, saturated fat and percentage of energy from fat and saturated fat when compared with traditional spoon-fed babies. Both groups had average calorie intakes that were higher than the estimated energy needs for babies of that age, and the average calorie intakes did not differ significantly between the two groups. So that's a good sign that baby-led weaners can get enough calories.

However, levels of iron, zinc, vitamin B$_{12}$, vitamin C, fiber and calcium were lower in the baby-led weaning group than in the spoon-fed group. Iron in the baby-led weaning group was less than half of the daily iron intake of the spoon-fed babies. Both groups received less than the recommended intake of iron, and 22% of babies consumed neither red meat nor fortified cereals. So while the baby-led weaning group wasn't lower in calories than the spoon-fed group, they were lower in some nutrients — an issue parents need to consider when following this method. The study recommended including foods that are rich sources of iron, zinc and vitamin B_{12} to counter these deficiencies. Meat is a great source of all three of these nutrients.

A 12-week pilot study by Cameron, Taylor and Heath (2015) tested the Baby-Led Introduction to SolidS (BLISS) method of introducing foods. BLISS follows the main tenets of baby-led weaning but, in addition, educates parents on safe practices for this feeding framework, including instruction on iron-rich and high-calorie foods, and choking prevention. The study found that the 14 babies in the BLISS group consumed 4.9 milligrams of iron per day through food. The control group of 9 babies, who were also using baby-led weaning but didn't receive any extra instruction on how to do so, consumed an average of 2.2 milligrams of iron per day. Compared to the standard baby-led weaning group, the BLISS group parents in the study were more likely to introduce iron-containing foods during the first week of complementary feeding. They were also more inclined to offer more servings per day of iron-containing foods when their babies were 6 months of age. This shows the importance of educating parents about how to successfully introduce solids using baby-led weaning, with a focus on iron.

A well-planned diet for your baby-led weaner will ensure that she gets adequate calories and fat, as well as necessary nutrients such as iron, zinc and B vitamins. The studies discussed above demonstrate that baby-led weaning (though often done in a way that can lead to nutritional deficits) can be a safe and enjoyable way to start your little one on solid foods. By knowing these facts, you have learned how to introduce important nutrients and foods into your baby's diet right from the start.

A well-planned diet for your baby-led weaner will ensure that she gets adequate calories and fat, as well as necessary nutrients such as iron, zinc and B vitamins.

Foods to Limit or Avoid

Technically, your baby can have anything to eat after 6 months of age, except honey (see below). But there are some foods that you may eat yourself that aren't the best choices for your baby. Here are a few of them.

- **High-salt foods.** Many restaurant meals and packaged foods are too high in sodium. From 7 to 12 months of age, your baby should get a maximum of 400 milligrams of sodium per day. When you're cooking at home, add most of the salt to the adults' servings once you've removed your baby's portion.

- **High-sugar foods.** Some sugar is okay, but get your baby used to eating plainer versions of sweet foods. Yogurt is a good example: choose plain full-fat rather than sweetened, and then add your own fruit. Note also that maple syrup and agave nectar are no better than regular sugar, even in small amounts.

- **Honey and products containing honey.** Avoid these, even if they are cooked. There's a small risk that they could cause botulism, a potentially fatal foodborne illness to which your baby is especially susceptible. There are a few hundred cases of infant botulism in the United States every year, which arise from ingestion of honey or contact with contaminated soil.

- **Cow's milk.** Avoid providing this as your baby's main source of milk until he is between 9 and 12 months of age — and at 9 months only if he is eating lots of solid foods. Some countries recommend waiting until 12 months in any case. Cow's milk is not as nutritious as breast milk or formula. If you continue to breastfeed, your baby won't need cow's milk.

- **Raw dairy and fish.** Skipping these will help prevent foodborne illness. Your baby is more susceptible to bad bacteria in food than adults are.

- **Low-fat foods.** Items in this category, such as fat-free yogurt or light cheese, aren't a good choice for little ones. Babies need lots of fat to grow.

- **Artificial sweeteners and colorings.** Sweeteners provide no nutritional value, and colorings have been linked to behavior issues in children.

- **Nutrient-poor food.** This category includes most packaged and fast foods, even those targeted at babies and toddlers. Your baby doesn't need the toddler frozen meals you can buy at the store. Each bite he eats should be nutrient-dense.

Choking Prevention 101

Choking is, by far, the number-one concern I hear about from parents, grandparents and health professionals when they start little ones on solids. Sometimes it can progress to anxiety — caregivers become so fearful that their babies will choke on solid foods that they don't even attempt baby-led weaning.

Thankfully, a lot of this fear can be alleviated by taking a good look at the research in this area and by getting educated about the difference between choking and gagging. Learning about safe textures and shapes of food to offer your baby and studying infant CPR are also critical when it comes to preventing and handling choking.

Research on Baby-Led Weaning and Choking

Exciting new research is helping to show that baby-led weaning can be as safe as traditional weaning. The Baby-Led Introduction to SolidS (BLISS) study (Fangupo et al, 2016) was a 2-year-long randomized control trial done in New Zealand. The authors compared a control group of traditional, mostly spoon-fed, babies with a group that was fed using the BLISS method, which combines regular baby-led weaning techniques with extra instruction on specific safety and feeding measures, such as choking prevention and offering high-iron foods.

Part of the study was designed to determine if the babies in the BLISS group experienced higher or lower rates of choking and gagging than spoon-fed babies. Questionnaires to assess gagging and choking frequency were given to parents when their babies were 6, 7, 8, 9 and 12 months of age. If the baby had experienced choking, parents were asked to identify the symptoms of choking, who resolved the episode, what food was fed and who fed the baby.

The study found that the number of babies who choked did not differ between the two groups, at any of the ages studied. Of the 170 babies who participated, 59 of them choked at least once (35%). Of the 59 who choked, three babies required medical attention — two had choked on milk, and one had

Take Care with Apples

Apples are the number 1 food that causes choking in baby-led weaners. It's important to never offer your baby a whole apple, but rather to peel it and slice it thinly, grate it or steam it until it's soft. See the Steamed Apple Wedges recipe (page 94) to learn how to prepare apples safely for your baby.

....

Gagging is a natural, healthy reflex. It closes off the back of your baby's throat and pushes the tongue to the front of the mouth so that any overly large pieces of food on it can be chewed further. Gagging is a regular part of the process of learning how to eat solids.

....

choked when the caregiver put food directly into the baby's mouth (which isn't recommended with baby-led weaning). These last three incidences go to show you that choking can happen on anything, not just finger foods.

In the study, gagging happened far more frequently than choking: 8,114 incidences were reported. More BLISS babies gagged at 6 months of age than their peers in the control group, who were traditionally weaned by starting on purées. By 8 months of age, the BLISS babies had the hang of eating solids and gagged less than the control-group babies, who were just beginning to eat finger foods. But while there was no increased incidence of choking in the BLISS group, the study authors pointed out that these results shouldn't be extrapolated and applied to non-BLISS versions of baby-led weaning, in which caregivers don't receive extra education. Other concerning findings were that many babies in both groups were offered choking hazards to eat, and infants were not always closely supervised when they were eating.

While the BLISS study is the strongest and most recent research on this topic, what do other studies show? A small survey (Cameron, Taylor and Heath, November 26, 2012) of 20 baby-led weaning moms found that 30% (six out of the 20) reported that their babies had choked at least once. However, in all cases, the choking was resolved without intervention, because the babies expelled the food on their own. The study authors questioned whether many of these occurrences were actually misidentified cases of gagging, rather than true choking. Four of the six moms could recall the food that caused the episode, and it was — unsurprisingly (see sidebar) — raw apple in all cases.

In another study (Cameron, Taylor and Heath, 2013), 199 mothers completed a survey online. Their babies were classified into three different groups: 8% were "adherent baby-led weaners," who strictly followed baby-led weaning techniques; 21% were "self-identified baby-led weaners," who used spoon-feeding at least half of the time; and the remaining 70% were classified as "parent-led feeding," or traditional spoon-feeding. Of the entire group of 199, 32.6% reported one choking episode. The majority of choking episodes were on whole foods, yet there was no difference between the different groups for proportion of babies who choked. The authors also hypothesized that, because parents find it difficult to distinguish between choking and gagging, some of the self-reported choking incidents were probably gagging that had been misinterpreted.

Gagging vs. Choking

Gagging is a natural, healthy reflex. It closes off the back of your baby's throat and pushes the tongue to the front of the mouth so that any overly large pieces of food on it can be chewed further. Your baby is likely to gag a lot when she's learning how much food she can manage at once — and possibly when she tastes food she doesn't like. Some babies vomit as a result of gagging, and that can be normal. Gagging is a regular part of the process of learning how to eat solids.

Gagging is very common, and not dangerous at all. In fact, it's the body's protective mechanism to prevent choking. The gag reflex in a 6-month-old is triggered farther forward on the tongue than it is in an adult, but moves back as your baby grows. By 8 to 9 months of age, babies gag significantly less than they do at 6 months. One study (Cameron, Heath and Taylor, November 2, 2012) found the average age at which babies can eat finger foods without gagging is 8.4 months. While some little ones have a more sensitive gag reflex than others, it decreases with time. A tip: If your baby gags, don't overreact — it may scare her and decrease her interest in eating.

Some experts have a theory that introducing solids via baby-led weaning may actually be safer than with purées. While research hasn't shown that baby-led weaners choke less than regular weaners, it can be helpful for your baby to be in full control right from the start. If she learns how to manage solids at an earlier age, when her gag reflex is farther forward in her mouth, it may keep her from choking later on.

Choking, on the other hand, is far less common than gagging. It occurs when a piece of food partially or completely blocks your little one's airway so she can't breathe. Babies make little to no noise when they're choking (as opposed to the retching noises that come with gagging). That is why it is *so* important to watch your baby while she eats. Sit facing her, and eat at the same time, keeping your eyes on her face. Don't sit her on your lap while she's eating, and definitely don't go off and do dishes or cook while your baby remains at the table on her own.

Did You Know?

Nothing Lasts Forever

They grow fast! Remember that everything is a stage that will pass. Whether she's constantly throwing food across the room, refusing to eat certain (or all) foods or gagging with every bite, your baby will outgrow these temporary behaviors.

Mom's Words of Wisdom

Janelle, mom of baby Eliana, found that "The gag reflex was terrifying. I kept telling myself that as long as the food comes back out, she is doing it right. She gagged a lot but never once did she choke. It took her about 2 months to learn to chew, which greatly decreased any gagging."

Know the Signs: Gagging vs. Choking

There is a visible difference between benign gagging and dangerous choking. And it's vitally important to be able to spot choking as soon as it occurs. Watch for these signals.

- **What gagging looks like:** Your child's eyes will water, her face will turn red, and she will make a retching movement as her tongue pushes out of her mouth. She may also vomit.

- **What choking looks like:** Children who are choking are often silent, though you may hear a small whisper or gasp, which can be an effort to communicate distress or an attempt to get air. Babies' lips will start turning blue if they are choking.

Safe Sizes and Shapes for Finger Foods

Did You Know?

Mesh Feeder Bags

These tools are okay for some foods that may be a choking hazard, such as fibrous pineapple or frozen blueberries. But use them sparingly, as your baby needs to touch his food and learn how to chew and swallow it, not just suck on it through a feeder bag.

In the baby-led weaning world, you'll often hear that you should start by offering your baby easy-to-grasp stick- or finger-shaped foods. The idea is that these are easier to pick up for 6-month-olds, who haven't yet developed their forefinger and thumb muscles enough to master the pincer grasp. But here's why I don't suggest that: your baby's windpipe is about as wide as the nail on his pinkie finger. If he bites off a chunk of a stick- or finger-shaped food and it gets past his gag reflex, then it is the perfect size to become a choking hazard. So what is a safer alternative for your beginning baby-led weaner? Slice the food thinly, like a potato chip, making sure it's thinner than the width of your baby's pinkie nail and long enough so your baby can pick it up and have the food sticking out of her palm.

Avoid round foods, such as grape tomatoes and hot dogs, and items that your baby could take a coin-shaped or round bite out of. Apples are a good example, and surveys show they are the most common food that baby-led weaners choke on (see sidebar, page 36). If you offer your baby a whole apple, he can take a bite that, if not pushed out by his gag reflex, could block his windpipe and cause choking. Instead, slice the apple into wedges that are thinner than the width of your baby's pinkie nail; they are very unlikely to cause choking. Once your baby has developed a pincer grasp, at around 9 months, you can use a box grater to grate apples and other hard fruits and veggies, such as pears and carrots. You can also slice them into small pieces that your baby can safely swallow without chewing, if you prefer.

Safe Textures for Finger Foods

It's also important to consider texture when offering safe foods to your baby. Soft foods can usually be brought back up easily into the mouth, even if your baby does choke on them. Harder foods get stuck more easily in a baby's windpipe and require extra help to be expelled.

Make sure to try finger foods before you serve them. If you can squish the food between your tongue and the roof of your mouth, then it's soft enough for your beginner baby-led weaner. Foods like ripe avocado and banana automatically pass the squish test.

Your baby's gums are quite strong, even without teeth, but it's still easier for her to mash soft foods between her gums and swallow them — tough or fibrous foods (such as steak) are much more difficult. Bonus: when your child mashes and swallows her food, it begins to break down in her mouth, allowing her to take in more of its nutrients. (Food swallowed whole and unchewed just passes through her intestinal tract right into her poop!) While it's not unsafe for your baby to swallow small pieces of food whole — it does offer a good source of fiber — chewing the food will result in better nutrient absorption.

By 12 months of age, your baby will have developed the pincer grasp and more advanced chewing skills, both of which will allow her to manage harder foods more easily. At 6 months, she can perform only a simple up-and-down munching motion, which doesn't easily break down fibrous or hard foods. As your baby grows and gets the hang of chewing and swallowing soft foods, you can start to offer some different textures. Once your baby can pick up small items, it's safest to cut her food up into bite-size pieces — no need for super-thin foods anymore.

Once your baby has progressed to bite-size pieces, you'll still have to be cautious with certain foods. But how long will you have to grate apples and finely chop meats? While you should avoid classic choking hazards, such as whole hot dogs, whole pieces of popcorn and hard round candies, until your child is 4 years old, other foods will depend on her skill level and practice. Generally, between 1 year and 2 years of age, your little one will have plenty of teeth, and will be able to chew and swallow her food with ease. If you feel she's ready for food of the same size and texture that you eat, give it a try and watch carefully to see how she does. I find that I still slice up tough fruits and veggies for my three kids, who are well past weaning age, because they are easier and more appealing to eat.

Did You Know?

Don't Pre-Chew

Some cultures have no access to puréed baby food, so adults pre-chew food for infants, to make it easier for them to chew and swallow. However, one study (Ogunshe et al, 2013) examined this method and determined that it isn't recommended, because the bacteria from your mouth can be passed to your baby and cause tooth decay or illness.

Did You Know?

Pace Yourself

Some babies shovel as much food as they can into their mouths. This means they can't chew it, and so they gag. Happily, this common phase is just temporary. If your baby is a shoveler, offer her only a few pieces of food at a time (or just one at a time) to slow her down.

How to Safely Serve Potential Choking Hazards

There are a number of foods that are not safe for your baby to consume as-is. Many of them are round or too hard, which are obvious choking hazards, but some are not as easy to identify. Here are some ideas on how serve these foods in a safer way for your baby-led weaner.

Food to Avoid As-Is	Why It's a Choking Hazard	How to Serve It Safely
Apples	Too hard and potentially an unsafe round shape (depending on bite size)	Peel and cut into thin potato chip–shaped slices and steam until soft. Once your baby has developed a pincer grasp, you can grate raw apple with a box grater.
Beans and other legumes	Unsafe round shape	*Chickpeas:* Peel off the skin and break each pea in half. *Kidney, pinto, white and other beans:* Smoosh flat between your finger and thumb, or mash and serve as a spread.
Bread	Too gummy or sticky	Serve toasted.
Celery	Too fibrous	Avoid until age 4.
Cheese	Potentially an unsafe round shape	Grate or cut into thin slices.
Citrus fruit, such as mandarin oranges, whole sections	Membranes are too tough	Peel off the thin membranes or serve in a mesh feeder bag (see sidebar, page 38).
Corn kernels	Unsafe round shape, if hard	Serve cooked and very soft, such as in a casserole.
Dried fruit, such as raisins or dried apricots	Unsafe round shape	Chop finely.
Hard raw vegetables, such as whole raw carrots	Too hard and potentially an unsafe shape	Slice thinly (no thicker than the width of your baby's pinkie nail), and roast or steam until soft. Once your baby has developed a pincer grasp, grate them raw on a box grater or cut into small pieces (again, no wider than your little one's pinkie nail).

Food to Avoid As-Is	Why It's a Choking Hazard	How to Serve It Safely
Hard round candies	Unsafe round shape	Avoid until age 4.
Leafy greens	Too tough to chew	You can serve leafy greens, such as kale, baked into chips, or grind up spinach in smoothies.
Meat chunks	Too fibrous and tough	Slow-cook or pressure cook a rib or chicken leg your baby can grasp (remove any gristle), shred a slow-cooked or pressure-cooked roast, or offer cooked ground meat.
Nut butters	Too thick and gummy	Spread thinly on a slice of toast.
Nuts and larger seeds, such as pumpkin seeds	Unsafe round shape	Serve finely chopped or spread nut butters on toast.
Pineapple	Too fibrous	Avoid until age 4 or serve in a mesh feeder bag (see sidebar, page 38).
Popcorn	Unsafe round shape	Avoid until age 4 or break into small pieces, ensuring you're not serving any of the hard unpopped kernels.
Potato chips, corn chips and hard crackers (including rice crackers)	Too hard	Avoid until age 4.
Sausages and hot dogs	Unsafe round shape	Slice lengthwise into quarters.
Whole grapes, cherries, cherry or grape tomatoes, and large blueberries	Unsafe round shape	Slice lengthwise into quarters. Or squish soft large blueberries between your finger and thumb.

Top 10 Ways to Prevent Choking

Choking is not nearly as common as gagging, but it does happen to some babies whether you use baby-led weaning techniques or not. And food is not the only choking hazard. It's important to keep small objects out of your baby's reach, such as coins, marbles and buttons. The good thing is that you can take steps to prevent this frightening situation.

1. **Don't seat your baby on your lap to eat.** You always need to watch her when she is eating. Use a safe, good-quality high chair and sit next to her as you both enjoy your meal. Never leave the room to do dishes or prepare foods — a choking baby won't make any sound, so you won't hear her.

2. **Consider not buckling your baby into his high chair.** If he isn't at the climbing stage and can sit safely in his high chair without being strapped in, you will be able to get him out quickly if he needs some assistance clearing food from his throat.

3. **Don't offer choking-hazard foods.** Anything round, or that could be bitten off in a round shape, can block the windpipe and is dangerous when children are learning how to eat. Turn to pages 40 to 41 for a list of foods to avoid as-is, and how to prepare them so they are safer.

4. **Slice or grate foods.** Offer foods that have been sliced to prevent choking — they should be thinner than the width of your child's pinkie nail. Once your baby has mastered the pincer grasp, you can chop foods into small pieces or grate them.

5. **Offer soft foods.** These are easier for your baby to chew and cough back up if she gags. Test the foods before you serve them: you should be able to mash them between your tongue and the roof of your mouth.

6. **Never put a piece of food into your baby's mouth.** If he isn't controlling the food with his own tongue and chewing it, a piece may immediately fall to the back of his throat and block his airway. Give your baby full control and let him feed herself.

7. **Keep her seated.** Make sure your baby is sitting upright and not moving, running or crawling around. Don't allow her to eat in the car.

8. **Don't offer toys or TV while eating.** Your baby should concentrate on eating, without distractions.

9. **If he gags, let him handle it.** Know the difference between gagging and choking (see page 37). If your baby is gagging, don't interfere, dig for the food in his mouth or slap him on the back, which could lead to the food falling farther down his windpipe, causing true choking.

10. **Take an infant first aid class.** If your baby turns blue and doesn't make any noise, she could be choking — which is a life-or-death situation. If you have infant first aid skills, you'll be ready in the unlikely case you need them.

If your baby is gagging, don't interfere, dig for the food in his mouth or slap him on the back, which could lead to the food falling farther down his windpipe, causing true choking.

How to Respond if Your Baby Chokes

If you are positive that your baby isn't just gagging, your initial instinct may be to slap him on the back or to dig the food out of his mouth with your fingers. Unfortunately, both actions may force the food farther down his throat. If you can hear that he's getting in air — in other words, if he is wheezing or coughing — let him try to cough the food up on his own. If there's no air movement, pull him out of his chair immediately, start first aid and call 911 (get someone else to call if you're not alone).

Did You Know?

First Aid

It's important for everyone to have first aid skills. If you don't, attend a class. If you can't get to an in-person session, find an online course or, at the very least, watch infant first aid videos online. While you can avoid foods that have been identified as high risk, a recent study (Fangupo et al, 2016) found that only 23% of the foods that caused a choking episode in the study's participants had been on the author's list of high-risk foods — which means babies can choke on foods normally considered "safe." Since it's impossible to prevent all food-related choking, regardless of feeding method and foods offered, you need to have first aid skills to deal with dangerous situations if they occur.

How Much Food to Offer

Mom's Words of Wisdom

It's very common for your baby's appetite to go up and down. Noel says of her son Sam, "Yes, his appetite seems to vary a good bit, but we are still breastfeeding on demand, so I don't worry about it." Courtney says about her baby Elijah's appetite, "It differs. But I don't worry about it because if he doesn't eat, he has more milk. He only takes what he wants of everything."

Once you know what foods to offer (high sources of iron and calories, in safe sizes and textures), the next question is *how much* food to feed your baby. Luckily, there is a very easy answer: it's totally up to your little one!

Milk is your baby's main source of nutrition until about age 1. Weaning is all about balance; she will gradually decrease her milk intake as she eats more solids. Her caloric intake from breast milk or formula will decrease from 100% to 50% over the course of her seventh to twelfth months. By the end of that first year, about half of your baby's energy needs will come from table foods and half from milk. Remember, though, that this is a general guideline; some babies prefer solids to milk, and vice versa.

Dividing Up Responsibilities

Ellyn Satter, an international authority on feeding children, created a concept called Division of Responsibility in Feeding, which is published on her website, http://ellynsatterinstitute.org. It's a very helpful reference and, in my opinion, should be followed right from the beginning of starting solids. Her concept of feeding children works this way: you trust a breastfed baby to naturally take in the amount he needs, so you should trust an older baby to eat what he needs when he starts table foods. This theory meshes well with the main tenets of baby-led weaning, which encourage your baby to be in full control of feeding himself and taking in as much or as little as he desires. In fact, studies (including one by Brown and Lee, 2011) have shown that baby-led weaning parents pressure their children less to eat, and their babies are better at regulating their appetites according to their hunger.

Satter's division of responsibility identifies your roles this way: the parent chooses when, where and what the baby is offered to eat. The baby chooses if and how much he will eat.

By following your respective roles, your baby will grow up to have a healthy relationship with food. He will be less likely to be a picky or emotional eater, have an eating disorder or be overweight.

The Parent's Role
When

Babies up to about 1 year of age are fed milk on demand. But meals, when they begin, occur on a more regular schedule. There are especially big benefits of having structured eating times. Constant snacking prevents your child from building up an appetite for her meals, and she will end up consuming less overall. Following your little one around with food, trying to get her to take "just one bite" (a technique often used by parents of "small" babies) backfires, because she will never actually be hungry for meals. Aim for specific mealtimes, with a beginning and an end. When your baby shows signs of being finished, stop offering her food until the next meal or snack.

> **Constant snacking prevents your child from building up an appetite for her meals, and she will end up consuming less overall.**

Where

Your baby should sit in his high chair at the table and eat with the whole family. Family mealtimes are an important component of baby-led weaning not only because they are safer, but also because they offer a ton of benefits when your child grows into an adolescent (see Research Spotlight, below). Family meals are not just about the food — the connection and conversation you share are just as important. They're a beneficial habit to start from the beginning.

Research Spotlight

Family Meal Benefits

A study by Hammons and Fiese (2011) showed that adolescents who participated in family mealtimes not only consumed a more nutritious diet, but were also less likely to have an eating disorder or be overweight. Another study by Fulkerson et al (2006) determined that teens who ate meals with their families were also less likely to get involved in risky behaviors, such as using drugs or engaging in violence.

Safe Foods

If your baby resists trying new foods, you can have one "safe food" on the table: one that your baby would normally choose to eat if she's hungry. It can be as simple as bread with butter. This gives your baby the chance to have something to eat if she's really hungry but too stressed out to try a new food. Make sure to serve this safe food as part of the meal, rather than offering it as a backup if she refuses the rest of the meal.

What

You choose safe and nutritious foods to offer your baby. If she doesn't want it, that's her decision — respect it and don't be offended. Most likely she's just not hungry. Don't bring out a backup food you know your baby will eat ("She didn't eat dinner, but I know she'll eat this banana!"). Your little one will quickly learn that she doesn't have to try new foods because she can always wait and get her favorite. That's the perfect recipe for nurturing a picky eater. Don't become a short-order cook. Make a single family meal that's appropriate for everyone and leave it at that.

The Baby's Role
If and How Much

One of the most important things to understand is that your baby's appetite will vary — a lot. If you look at his growth chart, you'll notice that the curve isn't as steep after a year. Around this time, he stops growing so rapidly and therefore may start eating less. That often makes parents nervous, but it's normal. Other reasons for decreased food intake include sickness, teething (it hurts to eat) and excessive distractions. Most babies will increase their milk intake if they eat less, or will eat more the following week to compensate.

Parents often try to take over the child's role because they think it's their responsibility. It's *not* your job to "get" your baby to eat. It's your job to offer the food, and your little one's job to decide if he will eat it. If he's hungry, he will. Children are great at listening to their appetites, and parents should encourage them to maintain this skill as long as possible. And that can happen only if you fully trust your child to eat the amount he needs.

If your baby decides to eat nothing during a meal (or throughout a whole day), that's fine. We may not understand how babies can subsist on what seems like nothing more than air, but they do. If your baby is still growing along his growth curve, missing a meal or two isn't a problem. Only in very rare cases are babies not in tune with their appetites, and eat (or drink) less than the amount they need to grow.

Many parents pressure their children to eat using praise, rewards, bribes or punishments. Thankfully, once they know it's not their role, parents can relieve themselves of the burden of forcing the issue. Pressing children to eat backfires anyway, and they end up eating less. And not only that —

bribes and other forms of coercion can encourage emotional or binge eating, an excessive sweet tooth or an intense dislike of the foods they are forced to consume. Mealtimes become battlegrounds, full of stress and tears, instead of a peaceful place where the family can connect.

Think about Satter's division of responsibility: was it followed in your house when you were growing up? Did your parents allow you to choose how much to eat? Or did you have to take three more bites of broccoli, clean your plate or finish dinner before dessert? How does this affect you now? Quite possibly you still hate broccoli, always finish everything on your plate (even if you're full) or have a major sweet tooth.

How you deal with food around your child can affect him for the rest of his life. Start now, from the beginning of your child's relationship with solid food, to build good habits and feel confident that your child will eat the amount he needs. Your baby is the best judge of his own appetite.

The Right Growth Chart

Please make sure your doctor is using the World Health Organization (WHO) growth charts, which are specially designed for breastfed babies. They have been updated from the older Centers for Disease Control and Prevention (CDC) growth charts, which many health professionals mistakenly still use and can classify healthy babies as underweight. Remember that the 50th percentile is not the "goal weight" of your baby. Half of babies are naturally above the 50th percentile, and half are below it. Some babies are even above or below the weights on the chart. As long as they are following along their own curve, that's okay.

Tips for Babies Who Are Slow to Start

It's not unusual for babies to take a few weeks or even months to figure out how to eat — or to build up enough interest in eating to actually do it. Here are some ideas that may help, if you have a baby who's not too keen to put food in her mouth.

- **Let her play with her food.** One day she will squish it, the next she may touch it to her tongue, and maybe the next she will chew it and spit it out. Every step is progress, and a part of the process.

- **Eat together.** Sit beside your baby and offer him the same foods you have on your plate. Baby wants what Mom's eating, not his own baby food.

- **Make it easy to pick up.** Offer food in a size your baby can handle, and one that's easy to grasp when starting out. Make sure it has a soft texture so it's easy for her to bite off pieces and chew.

- **Keep your cool.** Don't pressure your baby to eat, or lose heart. Just keep on offering food and he'll get it eventually.

- **Let her do it herself.** Never put food into your baby's mouth. It can cause choking (see page 42) and she won't get practice feeding herself.

- **Go slowly.** Offer one food at a time. Your baby might get overwhelmed if he has too many choices in front of him.

- **Re-offer refused foods 15 times.** Your baby may need to see a particular food many times before she considers it safe enough to try.

- **Don't compare.** Babies are all different. Some eat a little; some eat a lot. It doesn't pay to compare your baby's habits against those of your friends' children.

- **Check his iron level.** If your baby isn't eating much by 9 months, it's a good idea to ask your doctor for an iron test. Low iron levels can cause reduced appetite and growth, so it's a bad cycle to get into — and low iron can be easily increased with supplements.

- **Review weekly.** Judge what your child eats on a week-by-week basis rather than a meal-by-meal one (or even a daily one).

Did You Know?

Ask an Expert

If your baby is slow to accept solids and seems to have trouble chewing, make an appointment with a speech language pathologist (SLP) or occupational therapist (OT) who specializes in feeding. Other reasons you may want to consider a feeding specialist referral: if your baby pockets food in her cheek, eats only specific textures, coughs or gags all the time, has a history of frequent colds, has a tongue or lip tie, or has an oral aversion (in other words, she doesn't put anything in her mouth, including toys).

- **Set up for success.** Place food on a familiar and well-loved mouthing toy and offer it to your baby. She may find this enticing.

- **Try nursing first.** If your baby seems angry or frustrated at mealtimes, maybe he is too hungry when you start. Try breastfeeding 30 to 60 minutes before bringing your baby to the table to try solids, so he has a bit of an appetite but isn't too ravenous.

- **Try a purée.** Finally, if your little one hasn't taken to baby-led weaning after a few weeks, you may need to be truly baby-led and see if she would happily accept a puréed food instead. Continue to offer finger foods for practice. This won't confuse or endanger your baby.

Signs of Hunger and Fullness

It's usually quite clear when your baby is hungry and interested in eating — and equally so when she is done with a meal. Below are some common indicators to watch for.

Signs of Hunger	Signs of Fullness
Reaching toward or pointing at food	Crying
Smiling at food and acting happy when food is presented	Throwing food
Acting alert and focused on food	Eating more and more slowly
Gesturing for more or for certain foods (this is especially helpful if you do baby sign language with your child)	Yawning or falling asleep
Licking lips and drooling	Squirming to get out of high chair

Don't Worry If Your Baby Is Bigger

Some babies are naturally bigger, and that is normal, too. Many have parents who are larger as well. Breastfed babies especially might have huge (and adorable) rolls, but those deposits of baby fat will not stick around for life and contribute to a little one becoming overweight as an adult.

It breaks my heart when I hear a mother say a health-care professional told her that her baby weighs too much and needs to eat less. If you follow Satter's Division of Responsibility in Feeding (see page 44) and don't force or overly encourage your baby to eat, then you're doing your job. There's no problem — no matter how much your baby weighs — if you're letting him listen to his own appetite.

Problems arise when you start restricting food. Two studies (Eneli, Crum and Tylka, 2008, and Satter, 1996) argue that if your baby still seems hungry after one portion of his meal, but you think he's had enough and don't give him another serving, he will learn to become obsessed with food and start to binge-eat. As your baby grows into a child with more freedom, he will eat as much as he can whenever he isn't restricted. For example, if Mom and Dad don't let him have seconds at dinner, a child doesn't know if he's going to be able to eat enough to satisfy his hunger, so he will binge or eat to excess at other times to compensate. This creates a very unhealthy relationship with food, and the child can end up weighing more despite the caloric restrictions.

> **Remember, your job is to provide a variety of (mostly) healthy choices at the table during structured meals and at snack times. From there, your baby or child takes over and your responsibility is done. If your baby wants more, feed him until he's showing you he's full and done eating.**

Remember, your job is to provide a variety of (mostly) healthy choices at the table during structured meals and at snack times. From there, your baby or child takes over and your responsibility is done. If your baby wants more, feed him until he's showing you he's full and done eating.

Preventing Picky Eating

Playing your role as parent, as outlined in Satter's Division of Responsibility in Feeding (see page 44), will go a long way toward preventing picky eating in your child. That said, some babies and children are just inclined to be more fearful of food. It's common around the age of 18 months to 2 years of age for a previously not-too-choosy baby to become more selective with her food preferences. Some of this appears to be genetic — I often get moms blaming dads for their picky children!

While it may be challenging, it's important to continue to trust your baby's appetite and offer foods without pressure, rewards, bribes or punishments. And, as I've said before, don't become a short-order cook or automatically offer your child a "backup" food you know she will eat after she has refused dinner. Here are some more tips for handling picky eaters as they grow.

1. **Repeatedly offer previously refused foods.** Do this at regular meal and snack times — without applying pressure to your child to eat them. It sounds counterintuitive, but in the long run, it will allow her to expand her palate and cultivate a lifelong taste for these previously rejected items. Never force the issue, because it can cause a lifetime hatred of specific foods.

2. **Get your child involved in preparing food.** Grow a garden (or even a windowsill pot) of vegetables. Visit a farmers' market with your child and talk to a farmer about how carrots grow. Together, pick out a new vegetable to try at the grocery store. Ask your child to wash the lettuce. Getting him involved in the process of raising, selecting and/or preparing food will make him eager to taste it.

3. **Try different cooking methods.** Kale can be baked into yummy chips, which are more fun. Try sweet potatoes baked, mashed or in french fry form. Some children prefer raw veggies, and others like them cooked until mushy. Keep trying until you find one she likes.

4. **Offer food when your baby is hungry.** Try offering foods, such as an appetizer at the beginning of a meal, when your child is hungriest. He may be more willing to give it a try if he's hungry!

5. **Give vegetables funny names.** Kids will eat more "super-sight carrots" than plain carrots. They're just more fun.

6. **Try dips or sauces.** Hummus or yogurt dip provides extra nutrients as well as appealing flavors to go with veggies and fruits. Cheese sauce on cooked veggies enhances their flavor.

7. **Stay neutral.** Don't use food to soothe your child when she is crying or keep her busy when she is bored. This trains her to be an emotional eater instead of someone who eats to satisfy hunger.

8. **Be a good role model.** I have a lot of clients who say, "My husband won't eat veggies." Then why would his child want them? Expand your palate — a little someone is watching you.

9. **Be patient.** This is the most important advice. Picky eating is a phase that most children go through. It's a part of learning how to become independent and say no. Most picky eaters will start to improve by age 5, so hang in there.

> **While it may be challenging, it's important to continue to trust your baby's appetite and offer foods without pressure, rewards, bribes or punishments.**

Food Allergies

Did You Know?

High-Risk Allergenic Foods

The most common foods that cause allergies are milk, eggs, fish and shellfish, tree nuts (such as almonds, cashews and walnuts), peanuts, wheat and soy.

Food allergies are another big concern for parents who are starting to give their babies solid foods. The good news is that allergies are less prevalent than most people think — only about 8% of children have a food allergy — and some of them are outgrown. You're probably wondering if you need to delay offering particular foods, how to offer potential allergens for the first time and what allergic symptoms look like. Here, you'll find everything you need to know about food allergies.

Allergy Research and Guidelines

Back in 2000, health organizations recommended avoiding the introduction of high-risk allergens to babies for the first 1 to 3 years of life. The theory was that infants and toddlers didn't have well-enough-developed guts or immune systems to tolerate allergenic proteins. Very soon after, research started coming out supporting just the opposite theory: that delaying allergen introduction may actually be harmful and introducing them early is best. And, amazingly, we saw that this updated hypothesis was true — in the 10 years after the 2000 guidelines recommended delaying allergen introduction, the incidence of allergies doubled!

In 2008, the American Academy of Pediatrics updated its position, recommending that babies avoid allergens only up to 6 months of age. Experts had learned that introducing these substances early could help promote tolerance and reduce allergy rates.

Allergy vs. Intolerance

In an allergic reaction, your body's immune system mistakes a protein in food as a foreign invader and launches an attack, which includes the release of histamines. The results are allergic symptoms, including rashes and vomiting. An intolerance is totally different, and often results from the absence of an enzyme needed to digest a specific food. For example, in lactose intolerance, your body doesn't have enough of the enzyme lactase, which is needed to digest the lactose in dairy products. This particular intolerance is rare in babies, as breast milk is naturally high in lactose. Symptoms of intolerance are mostly digestive, including gas, bloating and diarrhea. Allergic symptoms can be serious, but symptoms of intolerance are not life-threatening.

Peanut Allergy Guidelines

In early 2017, the National Institute of Allergy and Infectious Diseases (NIAID) in the United States issued new clinical guidelines specifically related to peanut allergies. These were endorsed by the Canadian Society of Allergy and Clinical Immunology as well. The guidelines suggest that, for most babies at low risk of allergy, peanuts should be introduced soon after starting solids, when your baby is developmentally ready. Babies with mild to moderate eczema should also start peanuts at around 6 months of age.

For babies with an egg allergy, severe eczema or both, it is recommended to have a peanut allergy test done before offering peanuts for the first time. Babies whose test results show a low risk of reaction to peanuts can try them in their doctor's office or at home, starting as early as 4 to 6 months of age. Babies whose test results show a higher risk of reaction to peanuts should see an allergy specialist before they are offered peanuts.

Like me, you might have read the new NIAID guidelines and thought "Introducing peanuts to the most at-risk babies at 4 to 6 months? Why so early?" It's important to know that, while the LEAP study (see Research Spotlight, page 54) supported introducing peanuts early, and the babies studied started the study between 4 and 11 months, the average age at which the babies started the study was 7.8 months — 4 months was on the low end. The babies studied in Israel, where there are very few peanut allergies, started peanuts at around 7 months of age, not 4 months.

On top of that, the current recommendations from the World Health Organization (and all government health organizations in developed nations) support exclusive breastfeeding up to 6 months of age, at which time babies can be introduced to solids along with continued breastfeeding. So then why the "as early as 4 to 6 months" statement for high-risk babies in the new guidelines? I don't know. Maybe the authors of the new guidelines were anticipating research showing that introducing high-risk allergens before 6 months is beneficial, but we don't conclusively know that yet.

For now, the question is: Are the new guidelines for introducing peanuts appropriate if you're doing baby-led weaning? Yes! For all babies, including those at high risk for an allergy, introducing peanuts at 6 months of age fits within these guidelines and is appropriate according to the most current research findings.

> For all babies, including those at high risk for an allergy, introducing peanuts at 6 months of age fits within the new guidelines and is appropriate according to the most current research findings.

Research Spotlight

Support for the New Peanut Guidelines

One study that supported the new 2017 guidelines for introducing peanuts was the Learning Early About Peanut Allergy (LEAP) study in the United Kingdom (Du Toit et al, 2015). The researchers noticed that Jewish children living in the United Kingdom (where recommendations were to avoid peanuts for the first few years) had 10 times the prevalence of peanut allergy compared with Jewish children growing up in Israel. In Israel, peanuts become a regular part of a baby's diet at around 7 months. Testing the hypothesis that introducing peanuts early might actually be beneficial, the LEAP researchers studied 640 babies at high risk for peanut allergy. Half of the babies were given peanuts for the first time at 5 years of age, and the other half were given peanuts regularly starting at between 4 and 11 months of age. At the end of the study, 17% of the children who had experienced delayed peanut introduction had peanut allergy, compared with only 3% of the children who started eating peanuts within the first year of life. These results helped solidify the knowledge that it's better to introduce high-risk allergens early to promote tolerance.

How to Introduce Peanuts

So what's the plan for introducing a baby-led weaner to peanuts? Peanut butter is an easy source, but it is very thick and has a gummy texture, so it can be a choking hazard. Try spreading a thin layer on a strip of toast or a pancake. Or try Peanut Butter Cereal Fingers (page 104).

For your baby's first attempt, give him a small amount to eat; once he's consumed some, remove the peanut-containing food. Wait 10 minutes before offering more of the peanut-containing food and watch for signs of an allergic reaction, such as a rash, vomiting or difficulty breathing (call 911 if this happens).

If you are really nervous about feeding peanut butter to your baby, you can rub a bit on his cheek. Wait about 15 minutes and then rub a bit on his lip. Wait another 15 minutes and watch to see if a rash develops. If it does, don't give your baby any more peanuts and ask your doctor for an allergy test. If there is no skin reaction, feed your baby small and increasing amounts of peanut butter.

You may feel more comfortable if you have baby liquid antihistamine on hand in case you see a reaction. Most likely, this won't happen — in which case you can give the peanut butter back to your little one and let him eat more.

After a successful introduction, continue to offer peanut butter a few times per week. You can also try adding finely chopped peanuts to muffins or putting a spoonful of peanut butter powder in smoothies. You can also try puffed peanut butter finger snacks, which you can find online or in stores.

You Don't Have to Wait 3 Days

You may have been told to wait 3 to 5 days before giving your baby each new food so you can see if she shows any signs of allergic reaction to the previous one. Thankfully, you don't need to do this. It would be practically impossible to introduce one food at a time at this extended frequency during baby-led weaning, especially if your baby is eating family meals.

Some babies are at higher risk for developing allergies. Some have a known food allergy, which puts them at higher risk for other allergies; some have a sibling or parent with a food allergy; and some have severe eczema, which is linked to allergic reactions. If your baby is in this category, you may want to wait 2 days after introducing a high-risk food before introducing another. For example, if you introduce eggs to your baby, wait 2 days before trying out dairy, fish, shellfish, wheat, tree nuts, peanuts or soy. In between attempts, you are free to start any other low-risk food.

If your baby has a mixed dish or a variety of new foods at one meal and then appears to be having an allergic reaction, act like a detective and try each of the ingredients individually on other days to find the culprit. Sometimes other things cause similar symptoms — it's possible your baby is teething (and therefore extra-crabby) or has a virus (causing vomiting after eating) and doesn't have allergies at all.

Allergic Reactions

These episodes are usually mild. In fact, they may not be allergic reactions at all — your little one may just be tired or popping a tooth. If you aren't sure whether your baby has reacted to a specific food, you can try it again and see. If you are sure your baby has had a mild reaction, there's a good chance he will outgrow his allergy; retry the food again every 3 months (and keep baby antihistamine handy). If your baby has a severe reaction (see table, page 56), avoid the offending food completely and consult an allergist for confirmation.

Did You Know?

What About Dairy?

Wait until your little one is 9 to 12 months old to give her cow's milk as a replacement for breast milk or formula — it is not as nutritious. From an allergy perspective, full-fat yogurt, cheese and milk in cereal, smoothies or cooking are fine for your baby to try as she's starting solids.

Did You Know?

Gluten Timing

You may wonder if waiting to introduce gluten will help prevent celiac disease. So far, most studies have shown that neither introducing gluten early nor introducing it late makes a difference in preventing the onset of celiac disease.

Many babies who have a milk or egg allergy will outgrow it by the time they are 5 years old. Unfortunately, shellfish, tree nut and peanut allergies are less likely to be outgrown, so your child may need to avoid these for life if allergies to them are confirmed.

Signs of an Allergic Reaction

These are the signals to watch for when your baby is trying new foods. Most symptoms will be mild, but it's advisable to be aware of the symptoms of severe anaphylaxis, as discussed below.

Location	Symptoms
Skin	Redness, bumps, swelling or rashes; these often occur around the mouth, where food has come into contact with the skin, but can spread to the body
Gastrointestinal system	Vomiting, diarrhea or pain (which often results in extra fussiness)
Respiratory system	Runny nose, watery eyes, sneezing, difficulty breathing
Cardiovascular system	Drop in blood pressure and fainting

Did You Know?

Try Everything Early — Except Honey

All foods can be introduced after a baby hits 6 months of age, even high-risk allergenic foods (see sidebar, page 52). This includes foods that contain gluten, citrus, strawberries, nuts and shellfish. Honey is the one food you need to avoid until your child reaches 1 year of age. It carries a small risk of botulism, to which your baby is more susceptible in her first year.

Anaphylaxis Is an Emergency

Serious allergy cases can cause anaphylaxis, a life-threatening allergic reaction. When this occurs, your baby's immune system overreacts to a protein in her trigger food. Her blood pressure can drop, breathing becomes difficult and her airway can close. While most allergic symptoms are mild, if you think your baby is having a severe reaction, it's an emergency. Call 911 or go to the nearest emergency department, and administer injectable epinephrine, if you have it (or baby antihistamine, if you don't). After the episode is resolved, you need to make an appointment with an allergist to confirm the cause, and then strictly avoid the allergenic food — permanently.

Vegetarian Babies

There are many valid reasons why people choose to become vegetarian, such as environmental sustainability, concern for animal welfare and health. If you are a vegetarian, you will have to decide whether you want to raise your baby vegetarian, too. Some vegetarian parents offer their children animal products and let the children decide whether to become vegetarian when they are a bit older. Others raise their babies vegetarian from the very beginning.

The wider the variety of foods you can offer your baby, the easier it is to meet his nutritional needs. The good news is that a well-planned vegetarian, or even vegan, diet can support healthy growth and development at any stage of life. However, there are some nutrients that you must pay particular attention to, to make sure that your baby is getting adequate nutrition.

Types of Vegetarian Diets

There are a number of different types of vegetarianism. Each omits certain animal foods, while plant-based foods are acceptable. There is a lot of gray area in terms of strictness, so these are just broad definitions.

Type of Vegetarian	Foods Allowed and Omitted
Lacto	Consumes dairy products, but no eggs or other animal products
Ovo	Consumes eggs, but no dairy or other animal products
Lacto-ovo	Consumes eggs and dairy products, but no other animal products
Pesco	Consumes fish, but no other animal products
Vegan	Consumes no animal products at all; the strictest vegans omit honey as well, and don't wear wool or leather

Important Nutrients for Your Vegetarian Baby

What type of vegetarian you are determines which nutrients are especially important for you to focus on getting from food and/or supplements. Some of the important nutrients for vegetarians to keep an eye on include protein, omega-3 fats, iron, zinc, calcium and vitamin B_{12}.

Protein

> Contrary to popular myth, it's not difficult to meet protein needs on a vegetarian diet.

Contrary to popular myth, it's not difficult to meet protein needs on a vegetarian diet. The amount of protein a baby needs varies a bit depending on her weight, but 7- to 12-month-olds need, on average, about 11 grams of protein per day. What does this look like? Let's say your 8-month-old drinks 2 to 3 cups (500 to 750 mL) of breast milk or formula every day; that alone will provide about 5 to 10 grams of protein per day. Lacto-ovo vegetarians can easily provide extra protein by offering eggs, cheese and yogurt. Sources that are suitable for vegans (and vegetarians, of course) include tofu and other soy products; legumes, such as beans and lentils; and nut and seed butters.

You'll often hear that plant proteins are "incomplete," because they don't contain all of the essential amino acids. (Animal protein does contain all of these protein building blocks.) However, if you give your child a variety of different plant-based proteins, she will get the full range of essential amino acids over the course of the day or week. Vegans need to be a bit more vigilant to offer a protein source at each meal, because some plant-based proteins are not as highly digestible as animal-based ones.

Did You Know?

Milk Alternatives

If you are not able to breastfeed your vegan baby, fortified soy milk infant formula is recommended until age 2. After age 2, fortified almond, hemp or coconut milk is fine, but these milk alternatives are not high enough in fat or protein for babies up to 24 months old. Some countries' feeding guidelines suggest that soy milk rather than soy formula is fine after 1 year of age, but it's best to consult with a dietitian. She can help you determine if your baby's diet is adequate enough to switch from breast milk or formula to a fortified milk alternative.

Sample Menu: Adequate Protein for Vegan Babies

The current recommended intake of protein for a 1- to 2-year-old is about 13 grams per day. However, a study by Mangels and Messina (2001) reported that 1- to 2-year-old vegans need 30% to 35% more protein per day than their non-vegan peers. This works out to 17 grams per day for a 1- to 2-year-old vegan. Is this easy to reach? Yes! The sample menu below contains more than adequate protein.

Meal	Foods	Protein Content
Daily milk intake	2 cups (500 mL) breast milk	5.4 g
Breakfast	½ slice toast 1 tbsp (15 mL) almond butter ½ orange	1.6 g 1.7 g 0.6 g
Snack	¼ cup (60 mL) edamame ½ apple	5.9 g 0.2 g
Lunch	*Wieners and Beans:* • ½ cup (250 mL) vegan browned beans in tomato sauce • ½ sliced veggie hot dog ½ cup (125 mL) sliced avocado	7.0 g 3.5 g 1.3 g
Snack	1 small carrot 1 mini pita 1 tbsp (15 mL) hummus	0.5 g 1.3 g 1.2 g
Dinner	*Tofu Stir-Fry:* • ¼ cup (60 mL) tofu • ¼ cup (60 mL) cooked mixed veggies • ¼ cup (60 mL) cooked brown rice	5.3 g 1.4 g 1.2 g
		38.1 g total

Omega-3 Fatty Acids

The omega-3 fatty acid docosahexaenoic acid (or DHA for short) is important for normal brain and eye development. The main dietary source of DHA is fatty fish. There are also plant sources of omega-3s, but they contain alpha-linolenic acid (ALA). Flax seeds, chia seeds, hemp seeds, walnuts and canola oil are all good sources of ALA. However, ALA isn't as useful to the human body, as very little is converted into brain- and eye-building DHA.

The good news is that there is a vegetarian source of DHA: algae. I recommend that vegetarians and vegans, who don't consume fish, take an algae supplement. This is especially important during pregnancy and breastfeeding, as some iron will transfer from mother to baby to potentially help with his brain and eye development, reduce the risk of preterm labor and decrease the chance that your baby will have asthma. Once your vegetarian or vegan baby has started solids, you can consider a liquid plant-based algae supplement for him, too.

Iron and Zinc

You've already learned that your baby needs plenty of iron in her diet to ensure healthy brain and body growth (see page 23). Plants contain only non-heme iron (see page 27), which isn't absorbed as well as the heme iron in meat. Plus, the absorption level of non-heme iron depends partially on the presence of inhibitors (like phytates) and enhancers (like vitamin C) in the diet. That's why it's especially important for vegetarians and vegans to pair a source of iron and a source of vitamin C at each meal.

There are plenty of suitable iron sources for babies who don't eat meat or fish, such as eggs (for ovo-vegetarians), tofu, edamame, beans, lentils and hemp seeds. You can also serve iron-fortified foods, such as meat analogues or fortified infant cereals. Try baking powdered infant cereals into finger foods for your beginning baby-led weaner — Fluffy Iron-Rich Pancakes (page 102), Peanut Butter Cereal Fingers (page 104) and Avocado Muffins (page 107) are all delicious options. Once your baby has developed a pincer grasp, try some of the fortified finger-friendly cereals in the baby-toddler food aisle of the grocery store.

The American Academy of Pediatrics recommends that breastfed babies take an iron supplement starting at 4 months of age until iron-rich foods are started. While this isn't a worldwide recommendation, you may want to ask your doctor if she thinks iron supplementation would be beneficial for your vegetarian or vegan baby. The answer may depend on other factors, such as if you practiced delayed cord clamping at birth (see sidebar, page 24), if your baby was born prematurely or if you had adequate iron levels during pregnancy.

Zinc is another mineral that is important to get from food. It is necessary for immune system function and normal growth and development of the brain. The main food source of zinc is meat, but there are plenty of vegetarian sources, including soy, legumes, whole grains, seeds and nuts. Lacto-ovo vegetarians can also get zinc from dairy products and eggs. If you focus on high iron sources for your baby, you will also be offering her good sources of zinc.

Phytates: An Absorption Inhibitor

Phytates, the storage form of phosphorus, are found in whole grains, nuts, seeds and legumes. They decrease the body's ability to absorb both zinc and iron, and have been called antinutrients. This decreased absorption is a problem for vegetarians and vegans, because their preferred sources of zinc and iron, such as legumes, are also high in phytates. But there is a simple solution: to increase the breakdown of phytates and help increase nutrient absorption, you can sprout your grains and legumes. There is plenty of information on how to do this — and recipes that use these sprouted ingredients — on the internet to help you get started.

Calcium

Calcium is necessary to help teeth and bones grow and stay strong. The recommended daily intake for calcium is 260 milligrams per day for 7- to 12-month-olds, but it jumps to 700 milligrams per day for 1- to 3-year-olds.

For lacto-vegetarians, meeting calcium needs is no problem, but it can be a bit more tricky for vegans. Vegetables that don't contain calcium binders, which reduce absorption, can contribute to the daily intake. These include kale, turnip greens and bok choy — about 50% of the calcium present in these can be used by the body. (As a point of reference, about 30% of the calcium in dairy products is absorbed.) However, many other vegetables contain lots of phytates and oxalates (another antinutrient), both of which inhibit calcium absorption. These include spinach, beet greens and Swiss chard — only about 5% of the calcium in these gets absorbed. So while it looks like they are good sources of this important mineral, just a fraction is available to the body.

Calcium-set tofu is another good plant-based source of calcium, as are fortified plant milks — these boast about 30% calcium absorption rates. But plant milks don't contain enough fat and protein, so they often aren't recommended for children until age 2. You may also be able to find fortified soy or coconut yogurt, but be sure to check that they have added calcium and vitamin D. White beans, almonds, sesame seed paste (tahini) and figs can also serve as vegetarian calcium sources, with about a 20% calcium absorption rate.

Did You Know?

Try Some Tofu

Tofu set with calcium sulfate is a source of iron and calcium. Try the tofu recipes in this book, including Crispy Baked Tofu (page 109), Tofu and Spinach Lasagna (page 164) and Tofu Scramble (page 120). Or blend soft tofu into a smoothie for your baby-led weaner.

Calcium Absorption Rates

Food	Amount of Calcium Contained in Food	Amount of Calcium Absorbed by the Body	Absorption Rate
Broccoli, ½ cup (125 mL) chopped (raw or cooked)	36 mg	22 mg	61%
Bok choy, ½ cup (125 mL) cooked	84 mg	42 mg	50%
Kale, ½ cup (125 mL) raw	50 mg	25 mg	50%
Turnip greens, ½ cup (125 mL) cooked	104 mg	52 mg	50%
Milk, 1 cup (250 mL)	300 mg	101 mg	32%
Tofu, set with calcium sulfate, ½ cup (125 mL)	138 mg	41 mg	30%
Almonds, ¼ cup (60 mL) sliced	57 mg	11 mg	20%
Figs, dried, 2 medium	27 mg	5 mg	20%
Sesame seed paste (tahini), 1 tbsp (15 mL)	20 mg	4 mg	20%
White beans, ½ cup (125 mL) cooked	69 mg	14 mg	20%
Beet greens, ½ cup (125 mL) cooked	87 mg	4 mg	5%
Spinach, ½ cup (125 mL) cooked	115 mg	6 mg	5%
Swiss chard, ½ cup (125 mL) cooked	54 mg	3 mg	5%

Vitamin B$_{12}$

Vitamin B$_{12}$ is an especially important nutrient for vegetarians and vegans, because it's found only in animal foods. Vegans who don't consume vitamin B$_{12}$–fortified foods or take a supplement will become deficient. Early deficiency can cause slow growth in infants and lead to anemia and nervous system damage. Lacto-ovo vegetarians need to be thinking about this, too — even if they consume 1 cup (250 mL) of milk and 1 egg per day, they won't hit their recommended daily intake.

Vitamin B$_{12}$–fortified foods include meat analogues, soy milk, breakfast cereal, some yeast extracts and nutritional yeast. Always be sure to check the label to make sure the product is, indeed, fortified. As an adult vegetarian, consume dairy, eggs or fortified foods three times a day to meet your daily requirement — or take a 10-microgram B$_{12}$ supplement every day. If you're vegan and breastfeeding your baby, it's vital to take a supplement to ensure that your breast milk will pass a sufficient amount of this vitamin on to him. Toddlers can take chewable or spray B$_{12}$ vitamins; aim for about 5 to 10 micrograms per day and talk to your doctor to confirm that you're giving enough. Excess vitamin B$_{12}$ not required by the body generally isn't harmful and leaves the body in the urine.

Did You Know?

Nutritional Yeast

Sprinkle vitamin B$_{12}$–fortified nutritional yeast on toast or steamed veggies, add it to a smoothie, use it as a base for dips, or stir a bit into sauces and soups. It tastes a bit like Parmesan cheese, so it's great on pasta or in vegan "cheese" sauces.

Frequently Asked Questions

As a dietitian, I get a lot of the same questions on baby-led weaning. Here are some of the most common ones, and the answers I share with my clients. The questions are organized under broad headings; if you're looking for a specific topic, turn to the index on page 221 to help you find answers to your questions.

Getting Started

Q: *Aren't solid foods just for fun while my baby is still nursing?*

A: There is one positive about the popular quote "Food before 1 is just for fun." When parents consider food optional, it takes the pressure off if their child decides she's not interested in solids. You can't (and don't want to) force your baby to eat. Much of learning to eat in that first year will consist of experimenting with different textures and tastes, and milk does make up the most important part of your baby's diet until about age 1.

However, solid foods are an important supplement to milk starting at around 6 months of age. Why? Many reasons: they offer extra calories to support your baby's rapid growth, they help your little one develop motor skills and increase her acceptance of new foods and flavors earlier on. There's also new research that supports the idea of introducing high-risk allergenic foods at around 6 months to protect against allergies (see page 52). But the main reason solids are recommended at 6 months is to ensure your baby gets enough iron (see pages 23 and 60), which supports growth and brain function.

> **New research supports the idea of introducing high-risk allergenic foods at around 6 months to protect against allergies.**

Q: *My baby is 4 months old; can I start baby-led weaning now?*

A: Milk is all your baby needs until he is developmentally ready to start solids, at around 6 months of age. It's unlikely that a 4-month-old will be able to sit up well, pick up food, bring it to his mouth and "munch" it — all of which are prerequisites for starting baby-led weaning. While you wait for your child to reach that point, it's a good idea to sit him at the table during meals to get him in the habit. To build his skills, give him a plastic spoon or a hard munchable food (see sidebar, page 22), such as a Parmesan rind, carrot (if your baby has no teeth) or rib bone. Just make sure he can't break a piece off and choke on it.

Did You Know?

Acid Reflux
Occasionally, babies younger than 6 months have acid reflux, which solids can help relieve. Your doctor can help determine if solid foods will help, and will likely recommend puréed food if so.

Q: *When and how should I offer that first meal?*

A: Early in the day is a great time to start solids. This will give you time to notice if your baby experiences any kind of allergic reaction. She'll also be able to get any extra gas or bubbles out of her tummy after eating and before bedtime. Offer solids about 30 to 60 minutes after a milk feeding so your baby isn't stuffed full of milk when she begins. You don't want her to be ravenous, either, or she will get frustrated when she can't feed herself quickly enough.

Place small amounts of one or two food items on your baby's tray (more may overwhelm her) and let her feed herself. For safety reasons, never place food directly in her mouth with your fingers (see page 42). Start with food she can pick up easily — she should be able to grasp it with enough sticking out of her fist to munch on. Foods that are shaped like a thick potato chip are ideal.

Q: *How often do I offer solids when we're starting out?*

A: Begin with one or two meals per day around 6 months, and move up to three meals per day by 9 months. If you feel like giving him more meals per day for extra practice, that's okay, as long as he's still getting plenty of milk. By 12 months of age, your baby will be eating three meals and a few snacks per day. A snack or two can consist of just milk, depending on his nap schedule, which is always changing at this stage.

How-Tos

Did You Know?

Placemats

If you're using a high chair that pulls right up to the table, you may want some kind of placemat or bowl that suctions to the table to keep the mess contained.

Q: What are the best tools for baby-led weaning?

A: While you don't need anything except somewhere safe for your baby to sit when starting baby-led weaning, there are a few things that are nice to have.

1. **High-chair mat.** Baby-led weaning is messy. If you have flooring that's difficult to clean, you will want to protect it somehow. My favorite mess-collecting mat is a hard plastic computer chair mat because it's so easy to wipe. Some parents spread a plastic tablecloth under the high chair and shake the debris off outside after a meal.

2. **High chair.** You want your baby to be safely positioned in her high chair when she eats. A lot of parents prefer a super-simple hard plastic high chair, because it's easy to clean. Make sure the tray (or table, if you're pulling her right up to the table) is between her belly button and nipple line. Place a folded towel under her bum if the tray is too high. Roll up tea towels and place them next to her body if she's leaning a bit, to ensure that she is well supported. You want her to focus her energy on her arms and mouth, rather than on trying to stay upright.

3. **Bibs.** At home, you can just take off your baby's clothes to avoid stains, but bibs are handy when you're out and about. Some parents like full-body ones that cover the baby's arms as well. (Food really splatters sometimes!) Bibs with a lip to catch dropped food can help prevent waste. Just pick the dropped bits out and return them to your baby's plate.

Baby toothbrushes make good dippers for foods like yogurt and oatmeal.

4. **Dippers or starter spoons.** Baby toothbrushes make good dippers for foods like yogurt and oatmeal. Look for ones that have bristles made of the same soft plastic as the handle. Flat-headed starter spoons with ridges are also available; they help keep food from falling off. When your little one is ready for a proper baby spoon, choose a soft one with a shallow head or bowl. Deep-bowled spoons require too much lip movement for beginners. A dull plastic baby fork may be easier to use because it can stab, whereas spoons require a more-difficult scooping motion.

5. **Food storage containers.** You will often have leftovers after meals. Some may be appropriate to save and serve at the next meal or on the following day. Small food storage containers are useful for these and for packing on-the-go food. I love glass containers because they are microwave-, dishwasher- and freezer-safe.

6. **Cups.** Occupational therapists who specialize in feeding recommend using open cups as much as possible for babies. They're messy but effective at building strength in the mouth and lip muscles. There are tons to choose from: ones that are angled with handles, others that are shaped like plastic shot glasses or play-set tea cups, and others that look like little travel mugs but function like open cups — without spilling!

Q: *When can I offer my baby a spoon?*

A: Most babies between 9 and 12 months old can start experimenting with utensils to feed themselves. Even before this, you can offer your baby a dipper (see opposite), such as a baby toothbrush with soft plastic bristles or a ridged baby spoon. He will learn to dip this tool into infant cereal, oatmeal, yogurt or mashed potatoes and get the food to his mouth.

Dippers and spoons are also great tools to offer your baby even before you start feeding him solids. Sit him at the table at mealtime, and let him chew on a plastic toothbrush or spoon. He will practice manipulating tools in his mouth and may reduce his super-sensitive gag reflex.

> Most babies between 9 and 12 months old can start experimenting with utensils to feed themselves.

Q: *How do I feed runny foods during baby-led weaning?*

A: Offer thinner liquids, such as a brothy soup, in a cup to drink if your baby has mastered this skill. For soups with chunks, such as minestrone, pick the soft veggies and finger-squashed beans out and place them on your baby's tray.

For thicker foods, such as yogurt, thick soup or mashed potato, offer your baby a dipping tool, such as a plastic toothbrush or ridged baby spoon, if she isn't ready to scoop with a real spoon. Bread sticks make delicious edible dippers, too. Most babies will learn how to use a real spoon by around 12 months of age.

Q: Can I feed my child both puréed and finger foods?

A: This is often called "mixed feeding." While baby-led weaning has been defined in some studies as 90% or more self-feeding of finger foods, many parents define it more strictly as 100% self-feeding. After 6 months, most babies can self-feed all their food. However, if your baby can't manage, it's okay to try mixed feeding. He won't be confused or at increased risk of choking, despite the many unfounded warnings delivered by militant baby-led weaners.

Q: How do I know if my baby is eating enough food?

A: If your baby is growing consistently along her growth curve, then she is getting enough calories — it doesn't really matter whether it's through milk or food. (However, you still need to ensure your child gets enough of certain nutrients, such as iron and zinc, from foods, before age 1.) It does take many babies a few weeks to get used to handling food and eating it, or even to become interested in trying.

If your baby isn't into it after a month or two of offering solids, you may want to get her iron levels tested, because low levels can decrease appetite. But under no circumstances should you pressure or force your baby to eat food. See pages 48 to 49 for helpful tips that might get your baby interested in eating.

Specific Foods and Beverages

Q: When can I offer milk and milk alternatives?

A: Cow's milk is fine in cereal or baking once your baby has started solids. However, in Canada, it's not recommended as your baby's main source of milk until he reaches 9 to 12 months of age. Some other countries recommend waiting until 12 months to offer cow's milk as a beverage. This is because milk doesn't contain certain nutrients (like iron) that breast milk and formula do.

> If your baby is growing consistently along her growth curve, then she is getting enough calories — it doesn't really matter whether it's through milk or food.

If your baby is eating plenty of solids and getting lots of iron from food, then he can start drinking cow's milk at 9 months old. If he isn't taking in much food, wait until at least a year to make the switch. At a year, offer a maximum of 2 to 3 cups (500 to 750 mL) of whole cow's milk per day, along with regular meals and snacks.

In Canada, milk alternatives, such as soy milk, almond milk and coconut milk, are not recommended as your baby's main source of milk until age 2. Some other countries say they are appropriate after age 1. Again, this depends on what your little one eats, as these milks are low in fat and protein. Consult with a dietitian to determine if your baby's diet is adequate enough to change from breast milk or formula to a fortified milk alternative.

Q: Is raw milk okay for my baby?

A: Unpasteurized, or "raw," milk is touted as beneficial because it contains healthy bacteria that is normally killed by pasteurization. However, it also contains unhealthy bacteria that is normally killed by pasteurization, too. Infants are at higher risk of getting sick from these bacteria, and can experience serious diarrhea and vomiting — even kidney failure, paralysis and death. From 1998 to 2011, 148 raw milk product outbreaks, including two deaths, were reported to the Centers for Disease Control and Prevention in the United States. The majority of those cases occurred in children. Raw milk is not worth the risk.

Q: How much water does my baby need?

A: From 6 to 12 months of age, babies do not need a lot of extra water beyond what is supplied in their milk. You don't want water to take the place of nutritious milk or food. You can offer 2 to 4 ounces, or $\frac{1}{4}$ to $\frac{1}{2}$ cup (60 to 125 mL), of water per day to your baby, at mealtimes, so she gets the hang of drinking from a cup. If it's hot out or your baby is constipated, you can give her more, up to a maximum of 8 ounces, or 1 cup (250 mL), per day.

Q: Can I feed my baby juice?

A: Babies don't need juice. Nobody does, really! It is basically just sugar with vitamins, and it can weaken your baby's teeth. It's always more nutritious to eat whole fruits and receive all of their nutritional benefits, including fiber.

Did You Know?

Breast Milk

If you're breastfeeding and continue to do so, your baby doesn't need any other milk. Your milk adapts and changes with your baby's age and is always more nutritious for him than milk from another mammal.

Did You Know?

Open Cups

Open cups are recommended over sippy cups because they are the best at encouraging your baby's oral motor development. Look for cups shaped like small plastic shot glasses or kids' play-set cups. There are other alternatives, both in stores and online, that mimic the action of open cups but won't spill (see Resources, page 220).

The only time I do recommend juice is when your baby is constipated. Prune, pear and apple juice contain a natural sugar called sorbitol, which draws water into the bowels, making poop easier to pass. Give your baby a maximum of $\frac{1}{2}$ cup (125 mL) per day if he experiences constipation.

Q: *How much salt can my baby have?*

A: Early exposure to salt can create a lifelong preference for it. While people do need some sodium in their diets, most get too much. High sodium intake later in life can lead to high blood pressure and heart disease. Also, your baby's kidneys have not developed well enough to efficiently filter out large amounts of sodium.

In Canada and the United States, there is no official upper limit on sodium intake for babies under 1 year of age. It is, however, recommended that 1- to 3-year-olds consume less than 1,500 milligrams of sodium per day. (Adults should consume less than 2,300 milligrams per day, or 1 teaspoon/5 mL of salt.) Some other countries have more stringent recommendations. In Australia, a limit of 1,000 milligrams per day is recommended for 1- to 3-year-olds. In the United Kingdom, the guideline is less than 400 milligrams of sodium per day for 6- to 12-month-olds and less than 800 milligrams for 1- to 3-year-olds.

There are some creative strategies you can try to keep your baby's sodium intake low. When you make a home-cooked meal, remove your baby's portion before adding salt. You can also use herbs to add flavor without adding sodium. When you're shopping, choose low-sodium or no-salt-added canned fish, beans, tomato sauce and sauces, and avoid packaged and restaurant foods, which are almost always too high in salt.

Q: *How much sugar can my baby have?*

A: The World Health Organization suggests it's best to keep added sugar to less than 5% of caloric intake for babies. Added sugar does not include the sugars found naturally in fruit or unsweetened dairy products, but rather the sugars added to flavored yogurt, baked goods and so on.

What does 5% of calories from sugar look like for a baby? You just need to do a bit of math. Many babies between 9 and 12 months of age consume about 300 calories a day from food, so 5% equals 15 calories derived from sugar. Since sugar contains 4 calories per gram, this comes to about 4 grams of added sugar per day, or about 1 teaspoon (5 mL) maximum daily for your little one.

Did You Know?

Read Food Labels

Be sure to read all food labels to determine how many milligrams of sodium each serving of food contains. Keep in mind that your baby is not likely to consume the full adult-size serving listed on the package.

Q: Can my baby digest grains?

A: It's a common myth that you shouldn't feed babies grains before age 1 or 2. The reason given is that, until that age, babies don't make enough amylase, an enzyme that digests complex carbohydrates. It sounds scientific, but it's not true (see Research Spotlight, page 72).

There are a few reasons why most babies *can* digest complex carbohydrates, despite lower levels of pancreatic amylase. First, isomaltase and glucoamylase, two other enzymes in the small intestine, help break down carbs so that their sugars can be used for energy. A study by Lee et al (2004) found that even fetuses have mature levels of these enzymes. Glucoamylase splits complex carbs into absorbable glucose molecules and is particularly important in infants who have low levels of pancreatic amylase.

Second, and very interestingly, it seems that once your baby samples complex carb–containing foods, her body responds by secreting more amylase. (One study found that the same thing occurs with protein introduction and trypsin, the enzyme that digests protein.) So it appears that, to some degree, the body adapts to what it is fed.

Third, breast milk contains salivary amylase, too. Normally, salivary amylase is inactivated once it reaches the stomach, due to acidic pH levels, but the type present in breast milk is not inactivated in the stomach and continues to work in the small intestine, helping the body digest the milk. This amylase also works on any solid foods the baby consumes, making it easier for her to digest carbs.

Q: Can my baby have gluten, and when should I introduce it?

A: Gluten is a protein found in wheat, rye and barley. About 1% of people have an autoimmune disorder called celiac disease, in which gluten harms the intestines. Babies who have a parent with celiac disease are at higher risk of having it themselves. Reviews have found that delaying the introduction of gluten doesn't lower the risk of actually developing celiac disease, but it can result in later development of the condition. The European Society for Paediatric Gastroenterology, Hepatology and Nutrition recommends that you avoid giving your baby large amounts of gluten in the first weeks and months after starting solids. However, the ideal amount to offer hasn't been determined.

Did You Know?

No Need to Fear Grains

The relatively recent anti-grains movement has issued some fear-inducing claims about grains being harmful, but studies have established few negative consequences of carbohydrate consumption for young children. The biggest worry appears to be the development of cavities, which is, of course, influenced by oral hygiene practices. But there's no hard evidence to prove that grain consumption has negative effects on nutrient levels, obesity, diabetes development or cognition. The best advice is still to offer your baby a varied diet that includes all of the food groups.

Fortunately, it's not hard to limit gluten when you start baby-led weaning. By focusing on providing enough iron, you'll be serving meat and alternatives and a variety of whole foods from all food groups. While some regular gluten-containing breads and pastas are fine for babies and adults alike, it's beneficial from a nutrient perspective to try grain alternatives, such as pastas made from lentils or black beans.

Research Spotlight

Amylase and Carb Digestion

Amylase is produced by the pancreas and is present in saliva. Salivary amylase kicks off carbohydrate breakdown, but very little digestion actually occurs in the mouth. The vast majority happens in the small intestine. Plus, salivary amylase is usually inactive by the time it reaches the stomach, due to the acidic environment.

Amylase is present in very low levels in newborns' saliva, but a study by Morzel et al (2011) showed that it increases in abundance when a baby is between 3 and 6 months old. An older study by Sevenhuysen, Holodinsky and Dawes (1984) noted that, by 3 months of age, babies had a full two-thirds of normal adult levels of amylase. So, lack of salivary amylase definitely isn't a problem for babies who are starting solids at 6 months.

In the small intestine, where most digestion occurs, the pancreas secretes pancreatic amylase, which breaks down long carbohydrate chains into digestible simple sugars. Two studies, by Gillard, Simbala and Goodglick (1983) and O'Donnell and Miller (1980), report that, while newborns have only about 3% of an adult's pancreatic amylase, this begins to increase when they are 7 to 8 months old. They don't reach full adult values until they are 5 to 8 years old. But evidence shows that even having limited pancreatic amylase doesn't stop carb digestion. Other enzymes are available to help do the job (see "Can my baby digest grains?" on page 71). Even when small amounts of complex carbs make it undigested to the large intestine, bacteria there ferment them, causing gas but still allowing them to be absorbed by the colon (Lee et al, 2004). This may be uncomfortable for your baby, but it's not dangerous. It can happen even to adults, with some of the carbohydrates found in legumes!

Q: *When should I try eggs? Peanuts? Dairy?*

A: Shortly after starting solids is a good time to offer high-risk allergenic foods such as peanuts, dairy and eggs (see sidebar, page 52). You don't want these to be your baby's first foods (concentrate on iron-rich options instead), but experts now recommend introducing potential allergens early rather than delaying them. Doing this can help your baby build up a tolerance and actually prevent allergies.

To introduce peanut butter, spread a thin layer of it on a slice of toast and watch carefully for any reaction after your child digs in. You can introduce whole eggs any time after your baby is 6 months old. For a beginner, fry the egg and slice it into pieces he can grasp. As for dairy, you can try full-fat yogurt or cheese as soon as weaning begins. Don't switch from breast milk or formula until your baby is closer to a year old; this isn't due to allergy concern, but because breast milk and formula are more nutritious than cow's milk. Turn to pages 52 to 56 for more information on food allergies.

> **Don't switch from breast milk or formula to cow's milk until your baby is closer to a year old; this isn't due to allergy concern, but because it's less nutritious.**

Nutrients

Q: *Does my baby need supplements?*

A: The recommendations for supplementing babies vary by country. In the United States and Canada, it's recommended to give babies 400 IU vitamin D supplements starting at birth. In the winter in northern countries, where there isn't enough sunlight to supply your daily quota of vitamin D, you should continue to give supplements every year — even adults should take them! In the United Kingdom, the U.K. Department of Health recommends that children aged 6 months to 5 years be given a supplement containing vitamins A, C and D.

Q: *How much should I worry about iron?*

A: At about 6 months of age, your baby's iron stores, which were built up before birth, start to run out. The recommended daily intake for iron increases from 0.27 milligrams (the amount your baby gets from breast milk) between 0 and 6 months of age to 11 milligrams per day from 7 to 12 months of age. About 30% of

1-year-olds are iron deficient, so this is a common concern. If iron deficiency progresses to anemia, there can be irreversible consequences, such as learning difficulties and social withdrawal.

To make sure your baby gets the iron he needs, offer one of these options at each meal:

1. **Red meat, chicken or seafood.** These contain heme iron (see page 26), which is the easiest form for our bodies to absorb. For baby-led weaners, offer tender cooked meats, such as ground meat in sauce, meatballs, shredded slow-cooked roasts, meat loaf, ribs, chicken drumsticks or puréed cooked meat spread on toast.

2. **Eggs, beans or other legumes, leafy greens or dried fruits.** These contain non-heme iron (see page 27). For baby-led weaners, offer strips of fried egg, scrambled eggs and bean dips, blend leafy greens into smoothies and sauces, and add chopped dried fruits to baked goods.

3. **Iron-fortified cereal.** For baby-led weaning, you can bake infant cereal into foods such as pancakes; just substitute the cereal for half of the flour. As your baby develops a pincer grasp, you can offer iron-fortified toasted oat cereal O's.

Did You Know?

B$_{12}$ Supplement
Vegan children need a vitamin B$_{12}$ supplement. Consult a dietitian, who can help develop a diet and supplement plan (if needed) for your vegan or vegetarian baby.

Troubleshooting

Q: Why did my health professional discourage baby-led weaning? How do I respond?

A: This is a major concern for many parents who choose baby-led weaning. Maybe your mom or doctor hasn't heard much about it, and doesn't think it's a safe idea.

First off, share some of the benefits of baby-led weaning you've learned in this book (see pages 10 to 15), such as developing your baby's dexterity earlier, helping her achieve and maintain a healthy weight, and giving her full control so she develops a healthy relationship with food from the start. Baby-led weaning parents are less apt to pressure their children to eat and are less worried about their weight; parents and babies also find this process easy and fun.

Direct your critics to some of the studies listed in the References (page 218). There is more and more research coming out that explains the benefits of baby-led

Baby-led weaning parents are less apt to pressure their children to eat and are less worried about their weight; parents and babies also find this process easy and fun.

weaning. Some countries, such as Canada and the United Kingdom, now recommend offering finger foods at 6 months, when beginning solids. As even more research results are released, more health professionals will become comfortable with recommending this method. I believe it's far more useful for your health-care provider to teach you how to safely practice baby-led weaning than to simply say "Don't do it." By sharing the references in this book with him or her, you are helping move this process forward.

Q: *How do I deal with constipation?*

A: Babies often become constipated when they start eating solids. It may take a few months for your little one's intestines to adapt and figure out how to move food through efficiently. Constipation is not determined by the length of time between your baby's bowel movements. If your baby has hard, dry stools that are difficult and painful to pass, then he is constipated. Here's how to help.

- **Give him more fluids.** Increasing fluid intake is often the best strategy for promoting bowel movements. Give your baby a cup of water to sip with each meal and snack. If he won't drink from a cup or bottle, try a medicine dropper.

- **Try juice.** If water doesn't work, you can offer $1/4$ to $1/2$ cup (60 to 125 mL) of apple, prune or pear juice per day. These juices contain a natural sugar called sorbitol, which draws water into the intestines and makes poop easier to pass.

- **Offer a naturally laxative food.** Puréed prunes or Fruit Lax Spread (page 97) are good options. Ground flax seeds can help, too. Stir them into yogurt, add them to baked goods or roll your baby's avocado or banana slices in them.

- **Add probiotics.** These work for some babies. Talk to your doctor or pharmacist about adding probiotic powder or drops to your baby's food.

- **Reduce foods that are constipating.** You may find that certain foods make your baby's constipation worse. Fortified infant cereals, bananas and cheese are common culprits. Try taking these out of your baby's diet for a few days to see if it helps.

Mom's Words of Wisdom

Baby-led weaning mom Noel says, "I don't worry about what other people think about my parenting choices. My baby, my rules."

Common Baby-Led Weaning Myths — and How to Respond to Them

People have all sorts of opinions and responses when you tell them you're practicing baby-led weaning. Here are some of the common myths about this feeding practice, and how you can counter them with facts.

Myth: "Your baby will choke."

Response: "As long as I don't offer my baby choking-hazard-size food, he's unlikely to choke. You probably mean gagging — it's not the same thing as choking. My baby's gag reflex is close to the front of his mouth, and it actually protects him from choking. So now is a great time for him to learn to eat finger foods." (Also, if you took an infant CPR class, let your critic know that, in the unlikely case your baby does choke, you are trained in how to handle it.)

Myth: "Your baby can't get enough food if you don't offer purées."

Response: "Sometimes a spoon-fed baby gets too much food because it's easier for the parent to encourage her to eat more than she is hungry for. Plus, finger foods can be more nutrient-dense, as they aren't mixed with water. Most babies around 6 months of age or older can pick up food, get it to their mouth, chew and swallow it."

Myth: "Your baby can't get enough iron without infant cereal."

Response: "I can still offer my baby infant cereal without spoon-feeding him. I can bake it into pancakes he can pick up, or give him cereal with a dipper, such as a toothbrush, so he can feed himself. The iron in infant cereal isn't absorbed as well as the iron in meat, which I offer regularly. He also eats other high-iron foods at every meal."

Myth: "Your baby needs to learn to accept new textures gradually."

Response: "There's no research to support this. The more my baby can practice feeding herself finger foods, the better she will get at it and the more quickly she will adapt. Baby-led weaning helps her develop chewing and motor skills earlier than she would if she were spoon-fed. Learning to eat real foods at 6 months, when the gag reflex is far forward in the mouth, may also help prevent choking. At around 6 months, most babies are able to chew soft solids."

Myth: "Your family diet is not healthy enough/appropriate to feed your baby."

Response: "Baby-led weaning is a great motivation for us to improve our whole family's diet. I know how to alter our meals to make them more nutritious, and there's always something he can eat. If not, I have some basic finger foods at home that I can easily offer him, like eggs, beans and avocados."

Myth: "There's no research to prove that baby-led weaning is safe or healthy."

Response: "I can send you links from the research that has been done. There's a randomized control trial under way in New Zealand now to see if a specific method of baby-led weaning is healthy for babies. They've released some results, which found that the baby-led weaners in their study were at no greater risk of choking than traditionally weaned spoon-fed babies."

Myth: "Your baby needs food before she's 6 months old."

Response: "The World Health Organization, the American Academy of Pediatrics and Health Canada all currently recommend exclusive breastfeeding until a baby is 6 months old. I can send you the links to their guidelines."

Q: *My baby shovels food into his mouth and gags. What can I do to help?*

A: I had a baby like this, too. Some babies are just so eager to eat that they keep shoveling food into their mouths, and before long it's too full to chew or swallow. This is a phase that, like all phases, won't last long. In the meantime, I would suggest slowing him down by putting just one or two pieces of food on his tray at a time.

Q: *What if my baby gags a lot and even vomits after gagging?*

A: Some babies have a more sensitive gag reflex than others. The good news is that this is a natural preventive against choking. At 6 months, the gag reflex is triggered easily because it's located forward on the tongue, near the front of the mouth. By the time your baby is 9 months old, this trigger spot will have moved to the back of the tongue, resulting in less gagging.

If your baby vomits after gagging, don't worry. This is common, too. If it doesn't seem to deter your baby from eating, it's no big deal (other than being annoying to clean up). If your little one starts to become fearful of eating because it always causes vomiting, you may need to take a bit of a break from finger foods and try them again later.

Some babies have a more sensitive gag reflex than others. The good news is that this is a natural preventive against choking.

Q: My baby just plays with and throws his food. What do I do?

A: Most babies seem to do this around 9 to 10 months of age. It's just part of the learning process. If your floor is clean (and your dog doesn't snatch it), pick the food up and put it back on your baby's tray. Try feeding your baby less at one time — you'll waste less, and maybe she's just not hungry. Throwing food is often a sign that babies are done eating. Save leftovers in the fridge for another meal.

Q: How do I deal with the mess and wasted food on the floor?

A: Some babies do better using a tray with a lip, because they can't just sweep all their food over the edge. If he's eating at the table, pull him right up close to it, and try bowls or plates with suction cups that stick to the table. If you have a dog, the dog will certainly be grateful you chose baby-led weaning!

I like to put a hard plastic computer-chair mat (the kind you see in office-supply stores) underneath my baby's high chair because it's easy to wipe off. If you have a hardwood floor with grooves or carpet under your table, you will definitely need something like this. A soft plastic tablecloth can work, too, and it's easy to shake off after a meal. Just remember: even if you do all this, messes happen, and they're not unique to baby-led weaning.

Mom's Words of Wisdom

Janelle says, "My mother-in-law would take food away from my baby. I get it; in the beginning it was scary, because she gagged frequently. But I kept telling myself (and others) that I've watched friends' kids who were given baby food gag on solids. By skipping purées, my daughter was given food when her gag reflex was more sensitive. While that made it scarier for those of us watching, it was safer for her."

Part 2

Baby-Led
Weaning
How-Tos and
Meal Plans

Getting Started

Baby-led weaning is easy and fun for both parents and children.

Baby-led weaning means giving your baby real table food from the start, skipping right over the mush. Here, you'll learn the down-and-dirty of how to begin and progress with baby-led weaning. One of the best parts is that this process is easy and fun for both parents and children. So enjoy, and bon appétit, Baby!

When to Start: Is My Baby Ready?

Once you can check off the boxes on the list below, you're ready to roll with baby-led weaning. Remember, valid reasons to begin do *not* include "My baby is small and needs extra calories" or "My baby is big and needs extra calories." See pages 16 to 17 for more details.

Checkbox

❑ Your baby is 6 months old.

❑ Your baby has lost the extrusion (or tongue-thrust) reflex and doesn't automatically push solids back out of her mouth with her tongue.

❑ Your baby can sit up well in his high chair.

❑ Your baby has good arm and trunk strength. She can push up on her arms when lying on her tummy and is able to lean forward to grab or spit out food.

❑ Your baby can pick up foods with his palm.

❑ Your baby seems excited to eat and grabs at your food.

We're Ready! Nine Tips for Getting Started

1. Place small amounts of one or two food items on your baby's tray. Let her feed herself; don't put food in your baby's mouth (it can cause choking). Sit and enjoy your meal with your baby!

2. Start by offering food once or twice a day, early in the day. Your baby will be eating three meals a day by the time he's 9 months old. And by 12 months of age, he will be eating three meals and a few snacks (for a while, the snacks may be milk). But at the beginning, it's better to offer foods early in the day so he has a chance to work them through his system before going to bed for the night.

3. Work around milk feedings. While milk is your baby's main source of nutrition until she's about 1 year old, she won't have much interest in trying solids if you bring her to the table right after a milk feeding. On the other hand, if you wait too long afterward, your baby will be too hungry and may get frustrated at not being able to feed herself solids fast enough. Try offering them 30 to 60 minutes after a milk feeding, if the schedule works. That way, your baby will have some appetite, but not too much.

4. Start with soft food that has a "handle." At first, your baby won't be able to pick up smaller pieces. Instead, he will grab food in his fist but won't be able to eat the part in his palm. So he will start by eating down to his fist, then drop what's left and move on to the next piece. This means he needs food he can hold on to, and it has to be long enough to stick up out of his fist. Steamed broccoli florets have the perfect natural handle — no special prep! For other foods, cut them into a potato chip shape or into strips no thicker than the width of your baby's pinkie nail. Soft foods are best, because they are easier to cough back up if your baby gags. When he develops a pincer grasp, at around 9 months, you can offer smaller pieces of food that he can pick up between his thumb and forefinger.

5. How much your baby eats is up to her. If she's not interested in eating, that's okay. There's always the next meal (or day, or week!). Never bring out a favorite backup food, put food in your baby's mouth, pressure her to eat or reward her for eating. On the other hand, if your baby is giving you signs that she wants more food, that's okay too. You can feed her until she shows you she's had enough (see box, page 49).

Did You Know?

Getting Your Baby Ready

If your little one seems keen to start eating solid foods before he is 6 months old, or isn't quite ready at 6 months, put him on your back in a carrier while you cook. He'll experience the different, appetizing aromas of family dishes. Seat him at the table in his high chair during meals and offer him a spoon or teething toy to chew on.

If your baby has no teeth, offer him a hard munchable food (see page 22), such as a carrot, a Parmesan rind or a rib bone — something that will not break off in his mouth. Gnawing on these foods is good practice and will help him get ready to eat real food. It may also help decrease your baby's sensitive gag reflex.

6. Once your baby is 6 months old, all foods are good to go, with the exceptions of honey and choking hazards (see pages 56 and 40). Otherwise, you can offer him any food you like, including cheese, yogurt, wheat, eggs, peanuts and tree nuts, fish and shellfish. It's actually a good idea to introduce these high-risk allergenic foods soon after starting solids, to increase your child's tolerance — it may actually decrease his risk of developing allergies (see page 52).

7. Concentrate on serving iron-rich foods (see page 23). Your baby needs a lot of this mineral for healthy physical and mental growth in the second half of her first year. Offer an iron-rich food at each meal, along with a source of vitamin C (fruit or vegetable) to help increase absorption.

8. Your baby needs calorie- and fat-rich foods. For optimal brain development, he needs a higher percentage of fat in his diet than you do. Examples of high-fat foods include full-fat yogurt or cheese, meat, nut butters and avocado.

9. Become educated about the difference between gagging and choking (see page 37), then learn how to prevent and treat choking. Baby-led weaners are not at a higher risk of choking, but it's important for all parents to know what this dangerous situation looks like and how to handle it. See pages 42 to 43 for detailed information on choking prevention.

Meal Plans

While many parents start feeding their baby selections from family meals right from the beginning, others want to start a bit more slowly. They're looking for a concrete plan, which is just fine.

Starter Palmer Food Meal Plan

(6- to 9-month-olds)

This sample menu contains a full week's worth of starter foods for babies aged 6 to 9 months who are able to grab food with their palms. All of these meals offer a source of iron and a source of vitamin C, and supply plenty of calories and fat. Specific serving sizes for each item are not listed because it's up to your baby to decide how much to eat.

Day	Meal 1	Meal 2
Monday	Two-Ingredient Pancakes (page 101) with butter Pear slices	Spaghetti with meat and tomato sauce
Tuesday	Lentil Patties (page 108) Melon slices rolled in iron-fortified infant cereal or ground flax seeds (flaxseed meal)	Starter Pork Ribs (page 113) Beginner's Broccoli (page 98)
Wednesday	Beginner Eggs (page 100) with melted cheese Raspberries	Tasty Fish Cakes (page 168) Squash Fingers (page 98)
Thursday	Toast Fingers (page 103) with peanut butter Steamed Apple Wedges (page 94)	Quinoa Vegetable Cakes (page 139) Baby Avocado (page 95)
Friday	Baked Pear Breakfast Square (page 105) Baby Banana Strips (page 96)	Burgers for Beginners (page 111) Baby's First Sweet Potato Chips (page 99)
Saturday	Fluffy Iron-Rich Pancakes (page 102) with butter Raspberry Compote (page 97)	Slow-Cooked Pulled Pork (page 112) Crispy Kale Chips (page 194)
Sunday	French Toast Fingers (page 103) with butter and smashed strawberries	Tofu Burgers (page 110) Steamed Carrot Sticks (page 99)

Starter Finger Food Meal Plan

(9-month-olds and up, or babies who have developed the pincer grasp)

This meal plan is slightly more advanced. It's designed for a baby-led weaner who can use her thumb and forefinger to pick up smaller pieces of food, such as beans and grated apple. Most babies develop this skill at between 8 and 10 months of age and can also experiment with utensils. Three meals per day are included, because that is what most babies will be eating at this age and stage. Portion sizes are up to your baby. You can still feed milk on demand, and offer sips of water with meals.

Day	Breakfast	Lunch	Dinner
Monday	Finnish Apple Pancake (page 121)	Peanut butter and banana sandwich Grated carrot	Classic Beef Stew (page 185) Bun with butter
Tuesday	Toast with peanut butter Grated apple	Hamburger Pizza Buns (page 154) Bell pepper slices	Lentils Bolognese (page 159) on pasta Steamed broccoli
Wednesday	Scrambled eggs with cheese Buttered toast Berries	Creamed Salmon on English Muffins (page 143) Thin carrot slices with hummus	Turkey Sloppy Joes (page 179) on a bun Steamed cauliflower with cheese sauce
Thursday	Iron-fortified toddler cereal with milk Berries	Avocado and poached egg on toast Small apple pieces	Salmon with Roasted Vegetables (page 170) Pasta
Friday	Big-Batch Power Porridge (page 116)	Grilled ham and cheese sandwich Cucumber sticks	Simple Chicken Curry (page 176) Crispy Kale Chips (page 194) Rice
Saturday	Quinoa Kale Breakfast Casserole (page 127) Grated pear	Beef, Vegetable and Bean Soup (page 153) Yogurt with berries	Butternut Chili (page 163) Bun with butter
Sunday	Tofu Scramble (page 120) on toast	Crustless Mini Quinoa Quiches (page 149) Small pear pieces	Beef Pot Pie (page 186) Baby's First Sweet Potato Chips (page 99)

Snacks

By 1 year of age, your baby should also have regularly timed snacks every day. Sometimes it may just be milk, if naptime interferes. A nutritious snack contains at least two of the food groups. Check out recipes such as Chia Pudding (page 96), Peanut Butter Cereal Fingers (page 104) and Oatmeal Bites (page 106) and explore more ideas throughout the recipe section, which starts on page 91. If you don't feel like making lots of different recipes, stick to super-simple snacks that require minimal prep, such as cheese and sliced apples, or a hard-cooked egg and carrot sticks.

Drinks

Continue to breastfeed your baby on demand. Babies don't need much extra fluid beyond breast milk or formula. If you like, you can offer water — preferably in an open cup for muscle-building practice — at meals. It may help move the food along the digestive tract, if your baby is constipated. Limit water to about $1/2$ cup (125 mL) per day for babies under a year old. More than that can fill up his small tummy and make him less hungry for milk and food.

Your baby doesn't need juice. It's too high in sugar, and whole fruits and vegetables are healthier choices. If you make smoothies at home that include whole fruit, that's a better option. The one situation in which juice may be helpful is when your child is constipated. In that case, you can offer up to $1/2$ cup (125 mL) prune, apple or pear juice per day until the situation resolves.

> ### Did You Know?
>
> #### Solid Food Timing
> Bring your baby to the table 30 to 60 minutes after a milk feeding, if the timing works. This will ensure that he is hungry enough to be interested in food, but not so hungry that he will get frustrated by his slow eating pace.

Smart Choices by Food Group

Balanced meals contain all of the macronutrients: carbohydrate, fat and protein. Aim to offer two of the four food groups per snack, and at least three of the four food groups per meal.

Balanced meals contain all of the macronutrients: carbohydrate, fat and protein. When you're doing baby-led weaning, aim to offer two of the four food groups per snack, and at least three of the four food groups per meal. This will ensure that your baby gets a balance of the macronutrients, vitamins and minerals that she needs. Here are some tasty, nutrient-rich options from each food group.

Meat and Alternatives

- **Beans and legumes.** Drain and rinse canned beans to get rid of the salt. Black beans are easy to offer once your baby has developed a pincer grasp. For chickpeas, peel off the skins and split them in half. Squish kidney beans between your thumb and forefinger to make them a safe size for eating. You can also mash legumes to make spreads, such as bean dip or hummus.

- **Eggs.** Offer scrambled eggs once your baby's pincer grasp has developed. Until then, you can fry a whole egg and slice it into strips, or offer pieces of hard-cooked egg.

- **Fish.** Canned fish is really easy. Drained canned salmon with no salt added is a good choice (just be sure to pick out all of the bones first). Canned light tuna is low in mercury, but white tuna is not.

- **Meat.** Choose slow-cooked or ground meats, because they are tender enough for your baby to eat easily. A chicken drumstick or rib is good for your baby to grasp and will encourage him to self-feed.

- **Soy.** Firm tofu can be served grated or sliced into small cubes, on their own or to top a stir-fry. Soft tofu is great blended into smoothies. Shelled edamame (unprocessed soybeans) can be cooked until tender, either in the microwave or steamed on the stovetop. They are a good snack for a more advanced baby-led weaner who can pick them up.

Fruits and Vegetables

- **Soft fruits and veggies.** Avocado is an excellent choice, because it's high in nutritious fat and calories. Roll slices in fortified infant cereal, wheat germ or ground flax seeds to make it more graspable and boost iron content. This also works for banana. Round fruits and veggies, such as grapes and cherry tomatoes, still need to be quartered or sliced lengthwise, even though they are soft.

- **Steamed hard fruits and veggies.** Steam hard vegetables and fruits, like carrots, apples and unripe pears, until they are soft — you should be able to smoosh them easily between your tongue and the roof of your mouth. Avoid boiling, which causes vitamins to leach out of the food and into the water. For a beginner, slice the fruit or vegetable into thin strips; for a more advanced baby who can pick up small items, you can chop the food into small pieces.

- **Roasted veggies.** Roasting veggies makes them nice and tender and concentrates their natural sweetness.

> ### Did You Know?
>
> **Frozen Peas**
>
> Frozen peas are good finger foods and feel nice on the gums when your baby is popping a tooth. Serve them once your little one has developed a pincer grasp.

Grains

- **Toast.** Bread that has been toasted is less gummy, a texture that can be difficult for your baby to move around in her mouth and chew. You can remove the crust and cut the toast into "soldiers," or strips. Spread a source of fat, such as peanut butter or mashed avocado, on top for added calories and nutrition.

- **Iron-fortified toddler cereals.** Once your baby has mastered his pincer grasp, look for iron-fortified toddler cereals made without added sugar or salt. They're easy for your child to pick up and eat as-is, or you can serve them in milk to soften them.

- **Breadsticks.** Your baby can learn to feed herself oatmeal or other soft cereals with a dipper or a ridged baby spoon (see page 66). Breadsticks are a delicious alternative.

- **Well-cooked noodles.** Adults tend to eat pasta al dente, or when it's still firm to the bite. For babies, it's better to cook noodles until they're more well-done, so your toothless baby can easily mash them with his gums. Spiral noodles, such as rotini, are the easiest for your little one to pick up. Add a source of fat to the noodles, such as Parmesan cheese and olive oil, or melted cheese sauce, as your baby's fat needs are higher than your own, thanks to his rapid growth.

Milk and Alternatives

- **Cheese.** This is versatile and easy to serve plain, thinly sliced. Once your baby has developed a pincer grasp, you can shred it for her. Or melt cheese over steamed veggies or toast. Ricotta cheese is thick enough to eat with a spoon or dipper, and low-sodium cottage cheese can be picked up by more-advanced pincer grippers. Bocconcini is another good alternative, as it is soft and low in sodium.

- **Full-fat plain yogurt.** You can mix this with fruit or applesauce for flavor. Give your baby a dipper (such as a soft-bristled plastic toothbrush) or a ridged baby spoon to try out with it. Or serve it with a breadstick, which is a tasty edible dipper.

- **Full-fat cow's milk.** It's okay to add this to baked goods and cereal once your baby is 6 months old. Don't offer it as your baby's main milk source until he's closer to 1 year old.

Modifying Family Meals

One of the main tenets of baby-led weaning is offering family foods and eating together. Yet a small pilot study by Rowan and Harris (2012) found that only 57% of baby-led weaning families were actually eating the same meals. Perhaps, in those cases, the parents were not offering their babies the same food they were eating because they thought it wasn't appropriate in terms of seasoning — maybe they thought the meal was too spicy or salty. Or maybe the babies weren't yet physically able to feed themselves the items the rest of the family was eating, such as salad or small pieces that required a not-yet-developed pincer grasp.

Sometimes babies and parents eat different meals because Mom and Dad don't deem their dinners nutritious enough for Baby. Starting baby-led weaning is a great opportunity to take a closer look at your own diet. Do you often get takeout or fast food? Maybe you need to sign up for a meal-planning service or get organized so you can cook at home more often (and more easily). The desire to feed your baby well is great motivation.

Quick Baby-Friendly Modifications to Family Meals

There's a lot you can do to modify meals that you wouldn't automatically think of as baby-friendly. For the odd time when your meal isn't appropriate for your baby, keep these secret weapons in mind.

- **Soup:** If you're eating a chunky soup, pick out the pieces for your baby. If it's puréed or brothy, serve some in a cup to drink. Or let him try a spoon or breadstick to dip and lick.

- **Rice:** Roll it into a ball. This strategy is easiest with sticky rice.

- **Salad:** While your baby won't be able to eat lettuce and tough-to-chew greens, salads often have lots of toppings that are great for little ones; think chicken, avocado, egg, beans and veggies.

- **Spicy foods:** If you're having an extra-spicy chili or curry for dinner, rinse it in a colander to get rid of some of the sauce and spice. Or mix in some plain yogurt to cut the heat back. Spices such as turmeric, garlic, oregano and ginger are great for exposing your baby to different flavors. She likely won't appreciate too much chili powder or hot sauce at first, though!

- **Salty foods:** If your dish is too salty, place your baby's portion in a colander and rinse a bit of the sauce off. Or leave the salt out of a recipe and just add it at the table for adults who want it. Often spices give a dish enough flavor that extra salt isn't required.

- **Foods that require a spoon:** Think oatmeal, yogurt, applesauce or mashed potatoes. A breadstick is great for dipping and licking, as is a dipper (such as a soft plastic toothbrush) or a ridged baby spoon. He may also have better luck stabbing food with a fork than scooping it with a spoon. Babies tend to start using utensils at around 9 to 12 months of age; offer them often to encourage exploration.

....

If you're having an extra-spicy chili or curry for dinner, rinse it in a colander to get rid of some of the sauce and spice.

....

No matter what you're eating, there are benefits of sitting around the table and eating together as a family. I hope you feel like you have enough information to practice baby-led weaning with success. I know you will enjoy it as much as your baby will.

Mom's (Final) Words of Wisdom

Jessyka and baby Jonathan: *"Have fun with it! Take lots of pictures."*

Janelle and baby Eliana: *"The key is patience and trusting your instincts. And researching baby-led weaning."*

Heidi and baby Broxton: *"I was very nervous to try it at first (and when he gagged), but I would never change what I did. My son is a great eater who tries different foods and knows to chew (gum) his food and not suck it back and go straight to swallowing. It's messy but so fun!"*

Kayla and baby Brita: *"Baby-led weaning is so easy. They eat what you eat (within reason). As an exclusive pumper, I needed the next phase of her feeding to be simple. Spoon-feeding and purées seemed like more work, considering that she was able to eat regular food from the get-go with baby-led weaning."*

Noel and baby Sam: *"It can seem overwhelming at first, but once you get in the swing of it, you can't imagine feeding your baby any other way. It is wonderful when we go to restaurants, and he will try whatever."*

Part 3

Baby-Led Weaning Recipes

Recipes for Beginners

The 26 recipes in this chapter are nutritious and safe for your 6+-month-old baby. The only ingredient I've avoided is honey, as it is not safe until your baby is 12 months old. I've included some dairy, peanut and egg recipes, which are all great options to offer your baby soon after he starts eating solids. The recipes are as low in sugar and salt as possible. I've provided tips in some cases on how you can make the basic recipe tastier if adults or the whole family will be eating it.

The recipes in this beginner section are designed with the knowledge that your baby needs longer stick or potato chip–shaped foods to grasp, as opposed to small pieces. They are suitable for a baby who has a beginning palmer grasp.

Please let all heated food cool before offering it to your baby.

Steamed Apple Wedges

Makes 6 wedges

Apples are the main food that baby-led weaners choke on, so this recipe explains how to serve them safely. Because the slices are thin, you may have to help your baby pick them up at first, but she should be able to get each slice to her own mouth.

Tip

Once your baby has developed a pincer grasp, you can grate the whole apple (with peel) using a cheese grater.

- **Steamer basket**

¼	apple, peeled	¼

1. Using a paring knife or mandoline, cut apple into 6 wedges about ¼ inch (0.5 cm) thick.

2. Place the steamer basket in the bottom of a pot. Add water to the pot until it is almost touching the bottom of the basket. Cover the pot and bring the water to a boil over medium-high heat. Add apple wedges, cover, reduce heat to medium-low and steam for 2 to 3 minutes or until tender.

Nutrition Tip

Apples are an easy fruit to offer your baby and are available in all seasons. They contain vitamin C, so serve them along with a source of iron, like Slow-Cooked Pulled Pork (page 112).

Baby Avocado

Avocado is a great starter food for your baby, as it is soft and so easy to eat. But avocados are slippery and can be hard to grasp! To fix this, coat the avocado slices with infant cereal, wheat germ or ground flax. They will be much easier for your baby to handle.

Tip

Ripe avocados will yield to a gentle squeeze in the palm of your hand. If the avocado feels firm, it's not yet ripe. If it feels mushy, it is over-ripe.

½	avocado	½
2 tbsp	iron-fortified infant cereal	30 mL

1. Peel and pit avocado, then cut it into ¼-inch (0.5 cm) wedges (or no thicker than your baby's pinkie fingernail).

2. Place cereal on a small plate and roll the avocado slices in cereal to coat. Serve immediately.

Nutrition Tip

Avocados are high in calories and healthy mono-unsaturated fats, as well as fiber. Infant cereal offers an iron boost.

Variation

You can substitute ground flax seeds (flaxseed meal) or wheat germ for the infant cereal.

Baby Banana Strips

Banana is a nice soft starter fruit for your baby — there's no need to steam it! However, it can be a bit slippery for your baby to handle, so this recipe offers a solution.

½	peeled banana	½
2 tbsp	iron-fortified infant cereal	30 mL

1. Cut banana in half crosswise, then into quarters lengthwise.
2. Place cereal on a small plate and roll the banana strips in cereal to coat.

Tips

Some parents find that bananas cause constipation. If your baby becomes constipated after starting solids, avoid bananas for a while.

Since bananas are so soft, it can also be safe to cut the peel off the top half of the banana and leave the bottom half on for your baby to grip, instead of coating it in infant cereal.

Chia Pudding

Makes 1¼ cups (300 mL)

Chia seeds are high in omega-3 fats and thicken the coconut milk. For beginning weaners, this recipe provides a great slimy sensory experience to attempt eating with the hands! Later on, it can help your baby learn how to use utensils, first dipping and then scooping the pudding.

1 cup	coconut milk	250 mL
2 tbsp	ground chia seeds	30 mL

1. Stir chia seeds into coconut milk. Cover and refrigerate overnight to thicken. Stir well before serving to your baby.

Nutrition Tip

Besides omega-3 fats, chia seeds are high in protein and are a good source of minerals such as calcium, iron and magnesium.

Variation

Add berries or sliced fruit to the pudding, for extra flavor and nutrition.

Tip

Store leftover pudding in an airtight container in the refrigerator for up to 4 days.

Raspberry Compote

Feel free to use any berry or chopped fruit for this recipe, or a mixture. I like raspberries, as they provide a tangy flavor and bright color for your baby to experience.

2 cups	raspberries	500 mL
1 tbsp	water	15 mL
1 tsp	granulated sugar	5 mL

1. In a medium pot, combine raspberries, water and sugar. Cover and heat over medium heat for 10 minutes, stirring occasionally, until the fruit breaks down.

Tip
If fresh raspberries are not in season, you can use frozen berries. I keep large bags of fruit in my freezer throughout the winter. Not only is frozen fruit often more economical, but it is flash-frozen soon after picking, so it retains all of its nutrients.

Nutrition Tip
Serving the Fluffy Iron-Rich Pancakes (page 102) with this compote increases iron absorption, thanks to the vitamin C in the raspberries. And it adds flavor, too!

Fruit Lax Spread

Makes about 1¼ cups (300 mL)

This recipe is great for curing constipation. Spread it on toast or stir it into plain yogurt.

Tip
Refrigerate the spread in an airtight container for up to 1 month. Or fill an ice cube tray with the spread and freeze it, enclosing the tray in a freezer bag to prevent drying and freezer burn. Defrost each cube as needed.

- **Food processor**

½ cup	raisins	125 mL
¼ cup	pitted prunes	60 mL
¼ cup	pitted dates	60 mL
	Water	
6 tbsp	prune juice (approx.)	90 mL
¼ cup	wheat or oat bran	60 mL

1. In a medium bowl, combine raisins, prunes and dates. Add enough water to just cover the fruit (about 1 cup/250 mL). Cover and soak overnight.

2. In food processor, combine soaked fruit mixture, prune juice and bran; purée to the consistency of paste, adding more prune juice if the mixture is too thick.

Beginner's Broccoli

Broccoli is a great starter food, as your baby can eat it even before he has developed a pincer grasp. The stems serve as a natural handle!

Tip

You can also cook the broccoli in a microwave-safe steamer basket with 1 tbsp (15 mL) water. Microwave on High for about 4 minutes or until tender.

- Steamer basket

1	head broccoli	1
	Butter	

1. Cut broccoli into small florets, making sure each piece has a stem for a handle.

2. Place the steamer basket in the bottom of a pot. Add water to the pot until it is almost touching the bottom of the basket. Cover the pot and bring the water to a boil over medium-high heat. Add broccoli, cover, reduce heat to medium-low and steam for 7 to 10 minutes or until tender.

3. Transfer broccoli to your baby's bowl and top with 1 tsp (5 mL) butter per serving.

Nutrition Tip

Dark green vegetables like broccoli are among the most nutritious. Broccoli also contains lots of vitamin C, so it's great to serve with an iron-containing food to help absorb the iron.

Squash Fingers

Makes 25 fingers

Many different vegetables can be roasted into a soft french fry or potato chip shape. Here, I've used squash, but parsnips or carrots would work just as well.

Nutrition Tip

Butternut squash is a great source of vitamin A and has a nice mild flavor your baby will love!

- Preheat oven to 400°F (200°C)
- Rimmed baking sheet, greased

¼	butternut squash, peeled and seeded	¼
1 tbsp	olive oil	15 mL

1. Cut squash into thin strips about ¼ inch (0.5 cm) thick. Arrange in a single layer on prepared baking sheet and brush with oil to coat.

2. Bake in preheated oven for about 20 minutes or until tender.

Steamed Carrot Sticks

Makes 1 serving

Fresh local carrots have a natural sweetness your baby will love.

Tips

You can also cook the carrots in a microwave-safe steamer basket with 1 tbsp (15 mL) water. Microwave on High for about 3 minutes or until tender.

Once your baby-led weaner has a pincer grasp, you can grate a carrot with a cheese grater to serve raw.

- **Steamer basket**

$\frac{1}{2}$	carrot, peeled	$\frac{1}{2}$
1 tsp	butter (optional)	5 mL

1. Cut carrot into thin strips about 3 inches (7.5 cm) long and $\frac{1}{4}$ inch (0.5 cm) thick.

2. Place the steamer basket in the bottom of a pot. Add water to the pot until it is almost touching the bottom of the basket. Cover the pot and bring the water to a boil over medium-high heat. Add carrot sticks, cover, reduce heat to medium-low and steam for about 10 minutes or until tender.

3. Transfer carrots to your baby's bowl and top with butter, if desired.

Nutrition Tip

Carrots' bright orange color is thanks to beta-carotene, which is partially converted to vitamin A in our bodies. Vitamin A is an antioxidant and is important for eye health.

Baby's First Sweet Potato Chips

Makes 4 servings

Thinly slicing the sweet potato makes it easy for your beginning baby-led weaner to grasp the chips, yet they won't be a risk for choking.

Tip

Store the chips in an airtight container in the refrigerator for up to 4 days.

- **Preheat oven to 375°F (190°C)**
- **Rimmed baking sheet, greased**

1	medium sweet potato, peeled	1
1 tbsp	vegetable oil	1

1. Using a knife or mandoline, cut sweet potato crosswise into $\frac{1}{16}$-inch (2 mm) thick slices. Arrange in a single layer on prepared baking sheet and brush with oil to coat.

2. Bake in preheated oven for about 10 minutes or until chips are starting to brown and have softened, but are not crunchy yet. Transfer chips to a wire rack and let cool.

Nutrition Tip

Sweet potatoes are darker in color and therefore more nutritious than white potatoes.

Beginner Eggs

Eggs are one of the most nutrient-dense foods you can offer your baby. You can give him the whole egg any time after 6 months of age. This recipe will teach you how to prepare eggs so they are easy for your beginning baby-led weaner to handle.

- - - - - - - - - - - - - - - - - -

Tip

Once your baby has a pincer grasp, you can offer him scrambled eggs and mix in some cooked veggies and cheese.

| 1 | large egg | 1 |
| 1 tsp | butter | 5 mL |

1. In a small skillet, melt butter over medium heat. Crack egg into the pan, break the yolk and cook for 2 minutes. Flip egg over and cook on the other side to desired doneness. Remove egg from pan and cut into strips.

Nutrition Tip

Eggs are a great source of protein, as well as some hard-to-find nutrients such as choline and the antioxidants lutein and zeaxanthin.

Two-Ingredient Pancakes

Makes 8 pancakes

These are the easiest pancakes you will ever make! Feel free to get fancy with the suggested add-ins, but a mere two ingredients in the batter are enough to make a satisfying and nutritious finger food.

Tip
Leftover pancakes can be stored in an airtight container in the refrigerator for up to 4 days or in the freezer for up to 6 months. Reheat the pancakes by popping them in the toaster or microwave.

Nutrition Tip
Thanks to the eggs, these pancakes are high in protein and are a source of iron.

	Vegetable oil	
2	large eggs	2
1	mashed ripe banana	1

1. Preheat a large lightly oiled griddle or skillet over medium heat.

2. In a medium bowl, whisk eggs, then stir in banana.

3. Drop about 1 tbsp (15 mL) batter per pancake onto preheated griddle. Cook for 2 to 4 minutes or until golden on the bottom and beginning to bubble on top. Flip pancakes over and cook the other side until golden. Repeat with the remaining batter, adding more oil as needed between batches.

Variation
If you want to experiment, optional add-ins to the batter include one or a combination of: 1 tbsp (15 mL) ground flax seeds (flaxseed meal), 1 tbsp (15 mL) natural peanut butter, $\frac{1}{2}$ tsp (2 mL) vanilla extract or $\frac{1}{2}$ tsp (2 mL) ground cinnamon.

Fluffy Iron-Rich Pancakes

Makes 12 pancakes

These pancakes have a subtle coconut flavor thanks to the coconut oil. Coconut oil is high in lauric acid, a type of saturated fat that is also found in breast milk!

Tips

If your baby has troubles handling a whole pancake, cut it into strips.

Leftover pancakes can be stored in an airtight container in the refrigerator for up to 4 days or in the freezer for up to 6 months. Reheat the pancakes by popping them in the toaster or microwave.

Nutrition Tip

Simply by replacing some flour with fortified infant cereal, you are offering your baby a source of iron for breakfast!

	Vegetable oil	
½ cup	iron-fortified infant cereal	125 mL
½ cup	all-purpose flour	125 mL
2 tsp	baking powder	10 mL
1 tsp	granulated sugar	5 mL
¼ tsp	salt	1 mL
1	large egg	1
¾ cup	whole milk	175 mL
2 tbsp	melted coconut oil	30 mL

1. Preheat a large lightly oiled griddle or skillet over medium heat.

2. In a medium bowl, combine cereal, flour, baking powder, sugar and salt.

3. In a small bowl, whisk together egg, milk and coconut oil. Add to the cereal mixture and stir until well combined.

4. Drop about 2 tbsp (30 mL) batter per pancake onto preheated griddle. Cook for 3 to 5 minutes or until golden on the bottom and beginning to bubble on top. Flip pancakes over and cook the other side until golden. Repeat with the remaining batter, adding more oil as needed between batches.

French Toast Fingers

Makes 4 fingers

French toast makes an easy breakfast. It includes protein from the egg, and is soft and easy for your new baby-led weaner to eat.

Tips
The French toast fingers are great topped with Raspberry Compote (page 97).

In any recipe with milk, you can substitute pumped breast milk or formula.

	Vegetable oil	
1	large egg	1
1 tbsp	whole milk	15 mL
¼ tsp	vanilla extract (optional)	1 mL
Pinch	ground cinnamon (optional)	Pinch
1	slice bread	1

1. Preheat a lightly oiled griddle or skillet over medium-high heat.

2. In a shallow bowl, whisk together egg, milk, vanilla (if using) and cinnamon (if using).

3. Dunk bread in egg mixture, turning to soak both sides. Place on griddle and cook for 1 to 2 minutes per side, until golden on both sides. Cut into 4 strips.

Toast Fingers with Toppings

Makes 4 fingers

Your baby will have trouble eating a plain piece of bread, as it's so gummy. This recipe shows you how to offer bread in an easy-to-manage form, and provides ideas for nutritious toppings.

Nutrition Tip
Avocado will add healthy fat and vitamin E to your baby's toast. Peanut butter, hummus and cheese all provide protein.

1	slice bread	1

Suggested Toppings

Mashed avocado

Thin layer of natural peanut butter or hummus

Sliced cheese

1. Cut the crust off the bread and toast until lightly browned. Add desired topping and cut into 4 strips.

Peanut Butter Cereal Fingers

Makes 12 fingers

Soon after starting solids, your baby is ready to eat peanut products for the first time. This recipe is a good way to introduce your baby to peanut butter!

Tips

Look for a peanut butter with no added ingredients, such as salt or sugar.

Store cereal fingers in an airtight container in the refrigerator for up to 4 days. They can be served cold or warmed up in the microwave.

- Preheat oven to 350°F (180°C)
- Baking sheet, greased or lined with parchment paper

½ cup	iron-fortified infant cereal	125 mL
½ cup	natural peanut butter	125 mL
½ cup	whole milk	125 mL
1 tsp	ground cinnamon	5 mL

1. In a medium bowl, combine cereal, peanut butter, milk and cinnamon. Scoop up a 1-tbsp (15 mL) blob and form it into a stick about the same length as your index finger by rolling it between your palms. Place on prepared baking sheet and flatten with your hands to about ½ inch (1 cm) thick. Repeat with the remaining cereal mixture, placing the sticks about 1 inch (2.5 cm) apart.

2. Bake in preheated oven for about 15 minutes or until bottoms are lightly browned. Let cool on a wire rack.

Variation

You can substitute quick-cooking rolled oats for the infant cereal, if you prefer.

Baked Pear Breakfast Squares

....

This recipe is a tasty way to combine protein and iron from the egg with vitamin C from the pear.

• •

Tip

Store squares in an airtight container in the refrigerator for up to 4 days. They can be served cold or warmed up in the microwave.

Nutrition Tip

It's okay for babies to have some all-purpose flour. While whole wheat and whole-grain flours are more nutritious, they also contain lots of fiber, which will fill your baby up quickly.

• **Preheat oven to 400°F (200°C)**
• **8-inch (20 cm) square metal baking pan, greased**

2 cups	grated pears	500 mL
1 tbsp	melted butter	15 mL
3	large eggs	3
½ cup	all-purpose flour	125 mL
⅛ tsp	salt	0.5 mL
½ cup	whole milk	125 mL
Pinch	ground cinnamon	Pinch

1. In prepared pan, combine pears and butter, then spread evenly over the bottom of the pan. Bake in preheated oven for 5 minutes.

2. In a large bowl, whisk eggs. Stir in cooked pears, flour, salt and milk. Pour mixture back into pan and sprinkle with cinnamon. Bake for 15 minutes or until golden brown. Let cool in the pan, then cut into 16 squares.

Variations

Try grated apples instead of pears.

You can use any type of flour in place of the all-purpose flour.

Oatmeal Bites

These oatmeal balls are nice and soft, and are easy for your beginning baby-led weaner to grasp. Shape them into fingers, if you prefer.

Tip

Store the balls in an airtight container in the refrigerator for up to 4 days.

1 cup	quick-cooking rolled oats	250 mL
1 tbsp	ground flax seeds (flaxseed meal)	15 mL
1 tbsp	chia seeds	15 mL
1 tbsp	hemp seeds	15 mL
1 tbsp	natural peanut butter	15 mL
1 tsp	ground cinnamon	5 mL

1. Cook oats according to package instructions. Let cool.

2. In a medium bowl, combine cooled oatmeal, flax seeds, chia seeds, hemp seeds, peanut butter and cinnamon. Roll into balls about the size of golf balls.

Nutrition Tip

Hemp, flax and chia seeds are all high in fiber, protein and omega-3 fats.

Cheesy Breadsticks

Makes 20 breadsticks

Your baby can use these breadsticks as a dipper for some more difficult foods, like thick soup, yogurt, pudding or oatmeal.

Tips

Store breadsticks in an airtight container in the freezer for up to 6 months. Thaw in the microwave or at room temperature.

These breadsticks are a good on-the-go snack and an alternative to baby crackers or cookies.

- **Preheat oven to 350°F (180°C)**
- **Baking sheet, greased**

²⁄₃ cup	whole wheat flour	150 mL
²⁄₃ cup	all-purpose flour	150 mL
¹⁄₂ cup	butter, cut into cubes	125 mL
1 cup	shredded Cheddar cheese	250 mL
2	large eggs, beaten	2

1. In a medium bowl, combine whole wheat flour and all-purpose flour. Using a pastry blender or two knives, cut in butter until the mixture resembles bread crumbs. Stir in cheese and eggs. Bring together dough with your hands.

2. On a floured surface, roll out dough into a ¹⁄₂-inch (1 cm) thick rectangle. Cut in half crosswise, then cut into long strips about 1 inch (2.5 cm) wide. Place strips on prepared baking sheet.

3. Bake in preheated oven for about 10 minutes or until golden brown.

Avocado Muffins

Makes 35 mini muffins

These mini muffins are the perfect size for baby hands. The infant cereal adds some iron, the yogurt adds protein and calcium, and the avocado adds healthy fat.

Tips

Ripe avocados will yield to a gentle squeeze in the palm of your hand. If the avocado feels firm, it's not yet ripe. If it feels mushy, it is over-ripe (but still okay for this muffin recipe!).

Muffins are best within a day of baking them. Wrap extra cooled muffins individually in plastic wrap, then place them in an airtight container or freezer bag and freeze for up to 2 months.

- **Preheat oven to 375°F (190°C)**
- **35-cup mini muffin pan, lined with paper liners or sprayed with nonstick cooking spray**

1 cup	all-purpose flour	250 mL
½ cup	whole wheat flour	125 mL
½ cup	iron-fortified infant cereal	125 mL
2 tsp	baking powder	10 mL
½ tsp	baking soda	2 mL
½ tsp	salt	2 mL
1	avocado, peeled and pitted	1
½ cup	granulated sugar	125 mL
1	large egg	1
1 cup	plain yogurt	250 mL
1 tsp	vanilla extract	5 mL
½ tsp	ground cinnamon	2 mL

1. In a medium bowl, combine all-purpose flour, whole wheat flour, cereal, baking powder, baking soda and salt.

2. In a large bowl, using an electric mixer, beat avocado until smooth and creamy. Add sugar and beat well. Beat in egg. Stir in yogurt, vanilla and cinnamon until well combined. Pour in flour mixture, one-third at a time, stirring until just combined.

3. Divide batter equally among prepared muffin cups, filling them three-quarters full.

4. Bake in preheated oven for 12 to 15 minutes or until a tester inserted in the center of a muffin comes out with a few moist crumbs attached. Let cool in pan for 5 minutes, then transfer muffins to a wire rack to cool completely.

Variations

For full-sized muffins, bake in a 12-cup muffin pan for 25 to 30 minutes.

Gently fold 1 cup (250 mL) chopped berries into the batter at the end of step 2.

Lentil Patties

Makes 14 patties

Lentils are too small for a baby just starting out with baby-led weaning to grasp, but this recipe incorporates them into easier-to-handle patties. They can be served with plain yogurt, hummus or tzatziki to add moisture.

Tip

Store lentil patties in an airtight container in the refrigerator for up to 4 days.

Nutrition Tip

Lentils are an easy, inexpensive source of protein, fiber and iron.

1 cup	dried red lentils, rinsed	250 mL
3 cups	water	750 mL
2	large eggs, lightly beaten	2
$\frac{1}{2}$ tsp	garlic powder	2 mL
Pinch	salt	Pinch
Pinch	freshly ground black pepper	Pinch
1 tbsp	vegetable oil	15 mL

1. In a medium pot, combine lentils and water. Cover and bring to a boil over high heat. Reduce heat to medium-low, uncover and simmer for 5 to 7 minutes or until lentils are tender. Drain off excess water.

2. In a medium bowl, mash together lentils, eggs, garlic powder, salt and pepper. (Or, for patties with a smoother texture, blend the ingredients in a blender or food processor.)

3. In a large skillet, heat oil over medium-high heat. Drop 2 tbsp (30 mL) batter per patty into pan. Cook for 3 to 5 minutes or until golden on the bottom and beginning to bubble on top. Flip patties over and cook the other side until golden. Repeat with the remaining batter, adding more oil as needed between batches.

Variation

You can also use 2 cups (500 mL) canned green lentils, if you prefer. Just skip step 1, as canned lentils are already cooked.

Crispy Baked Tofu

Makes 4 servings

Tofu is a good starter food, as it's soft and a nutrient-rich meat alternative.

. . . .

Tips
Babies who have developed a pincer grasp can pick up cubes, whereas a younger baby with a palmer grasp will require the longer sticks.

This tofu can be used in any recipe that calls for purchased baked tofu. You can also use it as a substitute for chicken in any recipe or nibble it as a snack.

Store cooled tofu cubes in an airtight container in the refrigerator for up to 5 days.

• **Large rimmed baking sheet, lined with parchment paper**

16 oz	extra-firm tofu, drained	500 g
	Nonstick cooking spray	

1. Wrap tofu in four or five layers of paper towels. Place on a dinner plate. Cover with a second dinner plate. Place two or three heavy cans on top. Let drain for 30 minutes. Remove cans, plates and paper towels. Repeat process once more.

2. Preheat oven to 400°F (200°C).

3. Cut tofu into 1-inch (2.5 cm) cubes or 3- by 1-inch (7.5 by 2.5 cm) sticks (see tip). Spray all sides with cooking spray, then arrange in a single layer on prepared baking sheet.

4. Bake in preheated oven for 20 minutes. Turn cubes with a spatula and bake for 18 to 22 minutes or until golden brown and crispy.

Variation
The tofu can be tossed with a small amount of almost any herb or spice after spraying and before baking.

Tofu Burgers

Makes 9 burgers

These burgers, created by my friend Melissa from Wean Green, are mild-tasting, soft in texture and easy for your baby to handle. Tofu is high in protein and can also be a good source of calcium, if you look for one set in calcium salts.

Tips

You can use olive oil, canola oil or my favorite, avocado oil, to fry the burgers. Like olive oil, avocado oil is high in healthy monounsaturated fat, but it has a milder flavor and a higher smoke point (so you can cook with it at higher heats).

Store tofu burgers in an airtight container in the refrigerator for up to 4 days.

• **Food processor**

8 oz	firm tofu, broken into chunks	250 g
¼ cup	finely chopped onion	60 mL
¼ cup	fresh bread crumbs	60 mL
½ tsp	garlic powder	2 mL
1	large egg	1
1 tbsp	vegetable oil	15 mL

1. In food processor, combine tofu, onion, bread crumbs, garlic powder and egg; purée until smooth. Form into 9 patties, about ¾ inch (2 cm) thick.

2. In a large skillet, heat oil over medium-high heat. Cook patties, turning once, for 5 to 8 minutes per side or until browned on both sides and hot in the center.

Variation

For adults or older siblings, serve the tofu burgers on buns with your favorite burger toppings.

Burgers for Beginners

Makes 16 mini patties

These mini burgers are essentially squashed meatballs, so they're easy for baby's small hands to pick up and tender enough to chew.

· · · · · · · · · · · · · · · · · · · ·

Tip

Store burgers in an airtight container in the refrigerator for up to 4 days.

Nutrition Tip

Bison is a superstar when it comes to absorbable iron.

- **Preheat oven to 400°F (200°C)**
- **Rimmed baking sheet, lined with foil**

1 lb	ground beef or bison	500 g
½ cup	iron-fortified infant cereal, oat bran or wheat germ	125 mL
1	large egg, lightly beaten	1

1. In a bowl, combine beef, cereal and egg. Form into 16 meatballs. Place meatballs on prepared baking sheet, spacing them evenly, and press each meatball down into a small patty, about ¾ inch (2 cm) thick. Cover with foil.

2. Bake in preheated oven for 20 minutes or until no longer pink inside.

Variation

For more flavor, add a little bit of seasoning, such as garlic powder or dried oregano, basil or Italian seasoning, to the beef mixture. All seasonings (except salt) are fine for your baby, and exposure to different flavors early on may prevent picky eating later!

Slow-Cooked Pulled Pork

The slow cooker is a great tool for cooking meat for your baby. It keeps moisture in and ensures that the meat is nice and tender.

Tips

It's a good idea to freeze extras in individual portions, so you can warm some up if you're eating a family meal that's not appropriate for your baby.

If the whole family is eating this meal, feel free to add some barbecue sauce at the table. It makes a great pulled pork on a bun!

- **Minimum 3-quart slow cooker**

1	boneless pork shoulder blade roast (about 2 lbs/1 kg)	1
½ cup	ready-to-use low-sodium chicken broth	125 mL
½ tsp	garlic powder	2 mL

1. Place roast in slow cooker, add broth and sprinkle with garlic powder. Cover and cook on High for 4 to 6 hours or on Low for 6 to 8 hours, until fork-tender. With two forks, shred cooked meat. Discard excess liquid.

Variation
You can substitute a boneless beef chuck roast for the pork, and beef broth for the chicken broth.

Starter Pork Ribs

Makes about 13 ribs

Ribs are a good starter meat for baby-led weaners. These ribs are easy to grasp and nice and tender for your baby.

Tips

If the back of the pork ribs is smooth and shiny, the membrane has not been removed. To remove it, insert a sharp knife between the membrane and meat. Work your fingers under the membrane and peel it off.

It's a good idea to freeze extras in individual portions, so you can warm some up if you're eating a family meal that's not appropriate for your baby.

Nutrition Tip

Meat contains heme iron, the most easily absorbed type of iron. It's also a good source of zinc and vitamin B_{12}.

- **Minimum 3-quart slow cooker**

½ cup	water	125 mL
1	rack pork back ribs (about 2 lbs/1 kg), trimmed	1
½ cup	finely chopped onion	125 mL
1	clove garlic, minced	1

1. Pour water into slow cooker. Layer ribs in slow cooker, cutting into smaller portions if necessary, then top with onion and garlic. Cover and cook on High for 4 to 6 hours or on Low for 6 to 8 hours, until meat pulls away from the ends of the bones. Discard onion, garlic and liquid.

Variation

For the adults in the family, you can bake the slow-cooked ribs brushed with BBQ sauce in a 375°F (190°C) oven for 10 minutes while you wait for your baby's ribs to cool.

Family Recipes

· ·

One of the main benefits of baby-led weaning is that it allows you to make one meal for the entire family. You can sit and enjoy your meal along with your baby, rather than spoon-feeding her and then eating your own meal separately. Besides, babies are copycats and will probably prefer what everyone else is eating anyway!

The recipes in this section are great for your whole family, including your baby. They are lower in salt than most family recipes. While you do need to limit your baby's added salt intake, the majority of the salt in our diet comes from processed and restaurant foods. A small amount of salt in home-cooked meals is fine for your baby — you want the food to be tasty, after all! Feel free to add salt (or hot sauce) to your own plate to taste, after your baby's lower-salt portion has been removed.

The family recipes are also lower in added sugar than most, though for the sake of flavor I did not attempt to make them sugar-free. (Besides, most of the sugar substitutes, such as agave nectar, used in "sugar-free" recipes are no healthier than sugar.) However, none of the recipes contain honey, as it carries a risk of botulism for babies under 1 year.

Family meals are a great way to connect with each other while enjoying delicious food. Begin the habit of eating together when your baby is starting solids and, as much as you can, continue it as he grows. Adolescents who eat regular family meals enjoy a more nutritious diet, get better grades in school and are less likely to take drugs or drink alcohol.

I hope you enjoy these recipes as much as my family does!

Breakfasts

Big-Batch Power Porridge

Makes 18 servings

Your little one may start enjoying warm oatmeal for breakfast, along with Mom and Dad! Around 9 to 12 months of age, babies can start using spoons. If you're brave, let your baby eat the oatmeal with her hands — it's a great sensory experience!

Tip
Look for 9-grain cereal in the bulk food store or the bulk food section of your grocery store.

6 cups	large-flake (old-fashioned) rolled oats	1.5 L
1 cup	9-grain cereal (such as Red River)	250 mL
¾ cup	wheat germ, toasted (see tip)	175 mL
½ cup	oat bran	125 mL
½ cup	raisins or dried cranberries, chopped	125 mL
½ cup	sunflower seeds, chopped	125 mL

1. In a large bowl, combine oats, 9-grain cereal, wheat germ, oat bran, raisins and sunflower seeds. Store in a large covered container at room temperature for up to 1 week or in the refrigerator for up to 3 months.

2. To prepare 1 serving, bring 1 cup (250 mL) water to a boil in a small saucepan. Add ½ cup (125 mL) porridge mixture; stir and reduce heat to low. Cook, stirring occasionally, for about 5 minutes or until thickened.

Serving Idea
Add brown sugar (for the adults) and warmed milk; also delicious with a handful of blueberries.

This recipe courtesy of Konnie Kranenburg.

Toasted Quinoa Porridge

Makes 2 servings

With a slightly nutty taste and crunchier texture, quinoa offers an alternative to oats as a warm breakfast cereal.

½ cup	quinoa, rinsed	125 mL
1¼ cups	milk or plain non-dairy milk (such as soy, almond, rice or hemp), divided	300 mL
1 cup	water	250 mL
½ tsp	ground cinnamon	2 mL
⅛ tsp	salt	0.5 mL
	Chopped fresh or dried fruit	

1. In a small saucepan over medium heat, toast quinoa, stirring, for 2 to 3 minutes or until golden and fragrant. Add 1 cup (250 mL) milk, water, cinnamon and salt; bring to a boil. Reduce heat to low, cover and simmer, stirring occasionally, for about 25 minutes or until liquid is absorbed.

2. Serve drizzled with the remaining milk and with fresh or dried fruit, as desired.

Hot Millet Amaranth Cereal

Whole grains are high in magnesium, B vitamins and fiber. This recipe gives your baby (and the rest of the family) the opportunity to try some delicious whole grains — millet and amaranth — you may not have tasted before.

Tips

For best results, toast the millet and amaranth before cooking. Stir the grains in a dry skillet over medium heat until they crackle and release their aroma, about 5 minutes.

Unless you have a stove with a true simmer, after reducing the heat to low, place a heat diffuser under the pot to prevent the mixture from boiling. This device also helps to ensure the grains will cook evenly and prevents hot spots, which might cause scorching, from forming. Heat diffusers are available at kitchen supply and hardware stores and are made to work on gas or electric stoves.

2½ cups	water	625 mL
½ cup	millet, toasted (see tip)	125 mL
½ cup	amaranth	125 mL
	Milk or non-dairy alternative	
	Chopped dried cranberries, cherries or raisins (optional)	
	Toasted chopped nuts (optional)	

1. In a saucepan over medium heat, bring water to a boil. Add millet and amaranth in a steady stream, stirring constantly. Return to a boil. Reduce heat to low (see tip). Cover and simmer until grains are tender and liquid is absorbed, about 25 minutes. Serve hot, with milk or non-dairy alternative. If desired, sprinkle with cranberries and nuts.

> ### Slow Cooker Method
> Combine ingredients in a small (maximum 3½-quart) lightly greased slow cooker, adding ½ cup (125 mL) more water to mixture. Place a clean tea towel, folded in half (so you will have two layers), over top of the slow cooker to absorb moisture. Cover and cook on Low for 8 hours or overnight, or on High for 4 hours.

Local Veggie Scrambled Eggs

Eating solids is a great learning experience for your little one, using all of his senses. The bright red bell peppers and green asparagus in this recipe make a colorful dish for your baby to explore.

Tip

If you're short on time, you can use store-bought tzatziki instead of homemade.

8	large eggs	8
¼ cup	Homemade Tzatziki (see box)	60 mL
½ cup	crumbled feta cheese	125 mL
1 tsp	dried oregano	5 mL
½ tsp	freshly ground black pepper	2 mL
2 tsp	canola oil or butter	10 mL
½ cup	finely chopped green onions	125 mL
½ cup	chopped cooked potato	125 mL
½ cup	chopped roasted red bell peppers	125 mL
½ cup	chopped lightly steamed asparagus	125 mL

1. In a medium bowl, whisk together eggs, tzatziki, feta, oregano and pepper; set aside.

2. In a large nonstick skillet, heat oil over medium heat. Add green onions and potato; cook, stirring, for 4 to 5 minutes or until lightly browned. Add roasted peppers and asparagus; cook, stirring, until heated through.

3. Pour in egg mixture and cook, stirring with a wooden spoon, for 2 to 3 minutes or until eggs form soft, thick curds.

Homemade Tzatziki

Line a sieve with cheesecloth and set over a bowl. Pour in 2 cups (500 mL) plain yogurt (gelatin- and starch-free). Cover and refrigerate; let drain for 1 to 3 hours or until yogurt is thickened. Discard liquid in bowl. In a small bowl, combine drained yogurt, ½ cup (125 mL) drained grated cucumber and 2 cloves pressed garlic. Cover tightly with plastic wrap and refrigerate for at least 30 minutes or for up to 1 day.

This recipe courtesy of dietitian Mary Sue Waisman.

Avocado and Egg Breakfast Wraps

This recipe contains all four food groups and is a nutritious way for the whole family to start the day!

Tip

Hass avocados (sometimes called Haas avocados) are dark-skinned avocados with a nutty, buttery flesh and a longer shelf life than other varieties, making them the most popular avocado in North America. To determine whether a Hass avocado is ripe, look for purple-black skin and gently press the top — a ripe one will give slightly.

3	large eggs	3
Pinch	salt	Pinch
¼ tsp	freshly ground black pepper	1 mL
1 tsp	extra virgin olive oil	5 mL
3 cups	loosely packed spinach, chopped	750 mL
2 tsp	water	10 mL
2	6-inch (15 cm) whole wheat tortillas, warmed	2
2 tbsp	crumbled soft goat cheese	30 mL
½	small ripe Hass avocado, sliced	½

1. In a small bowl, beat eggs, salt and pepper until blended.

2. In a small skillet, heat oil over medium-high heat. Add spinach and water; cook, stirring, until leaves are wilted. Reduce heat to medium. Pour egg mixture over spinach. Cook, stirring gently with a spatula, for 2 to 4 minutes or until eggs are set.

3. Place half the egg mixture in the center of each warm tortilla and sprinkle each with 1 tbsp (15 mL) goat cheese. Top with avocado and fold or roll up.

Tofu Scramble

This tofu recipe is similar in texture to scrambled eggs! Tofu is a great vegetarian source of protein for your baby.

2 tsp	extra virgin olive oil	10 mL
1	large red bell pepper, chopped	1
1 cup	chopped mushrooms	250 mL
1	package (16 oz/500 g) extra-firm or firm tofu, drained and coarsely mashed with a fork	1
¼ cup	chopped green onions	60 mL
1 tbsp	low-sodium tamari or soy sauce	15 mL
Pinch	freshly ground black pepper	Pinch

1. In a small skillet, heat oil over medium-high heat. Add red pepper and mushrooms; cook, stirring, for 4 to 5 minutes or until softened. Add tofu, green onions and tamari; cook, stirring, for 5 to 6 minutes or until flavors are blended and tofu is golden brown. Season with pepper.

Sweet Potato Omelet

Makes 2 servings

The more colorful the fruit or veggie, the more antioxidants it contains! Sweet potatoes are high in antioxidants called carotenoids, to help keep you and your baby healthy.

2	large eggs	2
1 cup	shredded peeled sweet potatoes	250 mL
½ cup	chopped onion	125 mL
1	clove garlic, minced	1
1 tbsp	vegetable oil	15 mL

1. In a small bowl, beat eggs with a fork. Stir in sweet potatoes, onion and garlic until well combined.

2. Heat a medium skillet over medium-high heat. Add oil and swirl to coat the pan. Pour in egg mixture; cook, turning once, until lightly browned on both sides, about 2 minutes per side.

Tip
To flip the omelet, put a plate over the skillet and turn it out. Flip over into the skillet to cook the other side.

Serving Idea
This is tasty served with avocado, either cut into slices or mashed.

Variation
Substitute sliced green beans, chopped bean sprouts, finely chopped bell pepper, diced mushrooms or any combination of your favorite vegetables for the sweet potatoes.

This recipe courtesy of dietitian Nena Worth.

Finnish Apple Pancake

Makes 2 servings

This recipe is like a mix between pancakes and an omelet. The result is naturally sweet, thanks to the apples, with plenty of protein from the eggs.

Serving Idea

Serve with your favorite low-sugar fruit preserves.

- **Preheat oven to 425°F (220°C)**
- **8-inch (20 cm) square baking pan, g=**

2 cups	thinly sliced peeled apples	500 mL
1 tbsp	butter, melted	15 mL
3	large eggs	3
½ cup	milk	125 mL
⅓ cup	all-purpose flour	75 mL
¼ tsp	baking powder	1 mL
⅛ tsp	salt	0.5 mL

Topping

½ tsp	ground cinnamon	2 mL
1 tbsp	granulated sugar (optional)	15 mL

1. Place apples and butter in pan; toss to coat. Bake in preheated oven for 5 minutes.

2. Meanwhile, in a small bowl, whisk together eggs, milk, flour, baking powder and salt until smooth. Set aside.

3. *Topping:* In another small bowl, combine cinnamon and sugar (if using). Set aside.

4. Pour egg mixture over cooked apples; sprinkle evenly with topping. Bake for 15 to 20 minutes or until pancake is puffed and golden brown. Serve immediately.

umpkin Pancakes

Makes 18 pancakes

These lightly spiced pancakes are a delicious alternative to plain pancakes. Besides added flavor, the pumpkin also provides a bit of extra color and nutrition.

Tips

You can cook your own pie pumpkin to make the purée for this recipe or you can use canned pumpkin purée; just be sure not to use pumpkin pie filling, which is sweetened.

The chemical reaction of baking soda and vinegar makes this pancake batter particularly fluffy. Work quickly.

• **Preheat oven to 200°F (100°C)**

1 cup	all-purpose flour	250 mL
1 cup	whole wheat flour	250 mL
3 tbsp	lightly packed brown sugar	45 mL
2 tsp	baking powder	10 mL
1 tsp	baking soda	5 mL
1 tsp	ground allspice	5 mL
1 tsp	ground cinnamon	5 mL
½ tsp	ground ginger	2 mL
¼ tsp	salt	1 mL
1	large egg	1
1½ cups	milk	375 mL
1 cup	pumpkin purée (see tip)	250 mL
2 tbsp	canola oil	30 mL
1 tbsp	white vinegar	15 mL
	Nonstick cooking spray	

1. In a large bowl, combine all-purpose flour, whole wheat flour, brown sugar, baking powder, baking soda, allspice, cinnamon, ginger and salt.

2. In another large bowl, whisk together egg, milk, pumpkin purée, oil and vinegar. Add to flour mixture and stir to combine.

3. Heat a griddle or large nonstick skillet over medium heat. Spray lightly with cooking spray. For each pancake, pour ¼ cup (60 mL) batter onto griddle and cook for about 2 minutes or until bubbly around the edges. Flip and cook for 2 minutes or until golden brown. Transfer to a plate and keep warm in preheated oven. Repeat with the remaining batter, spraying griddle and adjusting heat between batches as needed.

This recipe courtesy of dietitian Karen Omichinski.

Weekend Wheaty Waffles

Adding some whole wheat flour increases the fiber and nutrition of these waffles, without compromising flavor! Store leftover waffles in the freezer, for an easy toaster-ready breakfast.

Tips

If your baby-led weaner has older siblings, get them to help break the eggs for the batter. With supervision, older children can help pour the batter onto the waffle maker.

To ease cleanup, be sure to wipe any spills off the waffle maker after making each waffle.

Depending on the size and shape of your waffle maker, the number of waffles you get from this recipe may vary.

Serving Idea

Serve topped with fresh berries.

This recipe courtesy of dietitian Kim Knott.

- **Preheat oven to 200°F (100°C)**
- **Belgian waffle maker, preheated to medium-high**

2 cups	all-purpose flour	500 mL
1 cup	whole wheat flour	250 mL
2 tbsp	baking powder	30 mL
2 tbsp	granulated sugar	30 mL
3	large eggs	3
3 cups	milk	750 mL
½ cup	canola oil	125 mL
	Nonstick cooking spray	

1. In a large bowl, combine all-purpose flour, whole wheat flour, baking powder and sugar.

2. In another large bowl, whisk together eggs, milk and oil. Add to flour mixture and stir until well blended.

3. Spray preheated waffle maker lightly with cooking spray. Pour ¾ cup (175 mL) batter onto waffle maker (or an amount appropriate for your waffle maker) and cook for 3 minutes or until golden brown. Transfer to a plate and keep warm in preheated oven. Repeat with the remaining batter, spraying waffle maker between batches as needed.

Banana Cinnamon Quinoa Waffles

Makes 10 waffles

Quinoa flour is simply ground whole quinoa, and you can find it in the health food section of your grocery store or make your own at home (see box). It adds an extra nutritional boost to this great finger-friendly breakfast recipe.

Tip

To store, let waffles cool completely on a wire rack, then wrap individually in plastic wrap and store in an airtight container in the refrigerator for up to 2 days or the freezer for up to 1 month. Reheat in the microwave on High for 45 seconds, until warmed through (no need to thaw), or toast in the toaster oven for 1 to 2 minutes or until toasted and warmed through.

• **Waffle maker, preheated to medium-high**

1¾ cups	quinoa flour	425 mL
¼ cup	ground flax seeds (flaxseed meal)	60 mL
1½ tsp	baking powder	7 mL
1 tsp	ground cinnamon	5 mL
¼ tsp	salt	1 mL
2	large eggs	2
1 cup	milk	250 mL
3 tbsp	unsalted butter, melted	45 mL
2 tbsp	pure maple syrup	30 mL
2 tsp	vanilla extract	10 mL
¾ cup	mashed ripe bananas	175 mL
	Nonstick cooking spray	

1. In a large bowl, whisk together quinoa flour, flax seeds, baking powder, cinnamon and salt.

2. In a medium bowl, whisk together eggs, milk, butter, maple syrup and vanilla. Stir in banana.

3. Add the egg mixture to the flour mixture and stir until just blended.

4. Spray preheated waffle maker with cooking spray. For each waffle, pour about ⅓ cup (75 mL) batter into waffle maker. Cook according to manufacturer's instructions until golden brown.

How to Make Quinoa Flour

Add ¼ cup (60 mL) quinoa to a high-power blender, coffee mill or spice grinder and pulse until finely ground. Repeat in these small batches until you have the amount of flour needed: 1 cup (250 mL) quinoa makes about ¾ cup (175 mL) quinoa flour.

Sweet Potato and Quinoa Breakfast Tortilla

Breakfast tortillas are a traditional Spanish dish. This one swaps the potatoes for sweet potatoes and quinoa, to provide extra nutrition for your family.

- **Preheat broiler, with rack set 4 to 6 inches (10 to 15 cm) from heat source**
- **Large ovenproof skillet**

1 tbsp	extra virgin olive oil	15 mL
2 cups	coarsely shredded peeled sweet potato (about 1 medium)	500 mL
6	large eggs, beaten	6
1 cup	chopped green onions	250 mL
1¼ cups	cooked quinoa, cooled	300 mL

1. In ovenproof skillet, heat oil over medium-high heat. Add sweet potato and cook, stirring, for 8 to 10 minutes or until softened. Add eggs, green onions and quinoa, gently shaking pan to distribute eggs. Reduce heat to medium and cook for about 8 minutes, gently shaking pan every minute, until eggs are almost set.

2. Place skillet under preheated broiler and broil for 1 to 2 minutes or until lightly browned. Slide out of the pan onto a cutting board and cut into wedges.

Spinach Quinoa Breakfast Bake

Makes 8 servings

Quinoa is often called a superfood. It is higher in protein, magnesium, iron, fiber and zinc than most other grains.

Tip

Make this ahead of time, let it cool completely, then cut it into squares. Wrap the squares tightly in plastic wrap and store in the refrigerator. The squares are delicious cold, but you can also zap them in the microwave to warm them up.

- **Preheat oven to 350°F (180°C)**
- **Blender**
- **8- or 9-inch (20 or 23 cm) square glass baking dish, sprayed with nonstick cooking spray (preferably olive oil)**

6	large eggs	6
2 cups	cottage cheese	500 mL
1	package (10 oz/300 g) frozen chopped spinach, thawed and squeezed dry	1
1¼ cups	cooked quinoa, cooled	300 mL
1 cup	chopped green onions	250 mL
1 cup	crumbled feta cheese	250 mL
⅛ tsp	freshly ground black pepper	0.5 mL

1. In blender, combine eggs and cottage cheese; purée until smooth.

2. Transfer purée to medium bowl and stir in spinach, quinoa, green onions, feta and pepper. Spread evenly in prepared baking dish.

3. Bake in preheated oven for 35 to 40 minutes or until golden brown and set.

Quinoa Kale Breakfast Casserole

Makes 8 servings

Kale is another superfood, high in nutrients such as folate. It can be difficult to incorporate kale into your baby's diet, as it's tough and chewy, but this recipe provides small pieces of soft kale that your baby can manage.

- Preheat oven to 350°F (180°C)
- 9-inch (23 cm) square glass baking dish, sprayed with nonstick cooking spray (preferably olive oil)

8	large eggs	8
1¼ cups	milk	300 mL
2 tsp	Asian chile-garlic sauce	10 mL
2½ cups	finely chopped kale (stems and center ribs removed)	625 mL
½ cup	quinoa, rinsed	125 mL
½ cup	finely shredded smoked Gouda cheese	125 mL

1. In a large bowl, whisk together eggs, milk and chile-garlic sauce until blended. Stir in kale and quinoa. Pour into prepared baking dish and cover tightly with foil.

2. Bake in preheated oven for 40 to 45 minutes or until just set. Remove foil and sprinkle with Gouda. Bake, uncovered, for 10 to 15 minutes or until golden brown. Transfer baking dish to a wire rack and let cool for at least 10 minutes before serving.

Flax Quinoa Date Muffins

These muffins are full of good stuff for your baby. Dark molasses contains iron, and flax contains omega-3s and is a natural laxative.

Tips

You can find quinoa flour in the health food section of your grocery store or make your own (see box, page 124).

Store the cooled muffins in an airtight container in the refrigerator for up to 3 days. Or wrap them in plastic wrap, then foil, completely enclosing them, and freeze for up to 6 months. Let thaw at room temperature for 2 hours before serving.

- Preheat oven to 350°F (180°C)
- 12-cup muffin pan, sprayed with nonstick cooking spray

1½ cups	quinoa flour	375 mL
¾ cup	ground flax seeds (flaxseed meal)	175 mL
1 tsp	ground cinnamon	5 mL
1 tsp	baking soda	5 mL
½ tsp	salt	2 mL
2	large eggs	2
1 cup	plain yogurt	250 mL
⅓ cup	dark (cooking) molasses	75 mL
1 tsp	vanilla extract	5 mL
1 cup	pitted dates, chopped	250 mL

1. In a large bowl, whisk together quinoa flour, flax seeds, cinnamon, baking soda and salt.

2. In a medium bowl, whisk together eggs, yogurt, molasses and vanilla until well blended.

3. Add the egg mixture to the flour mixture and stir until just blended. Gently fold in dates.

4. Divide batter equally among prepared muffin cups.

5. Bake in preheated oven for 22 to 27 minutes or until tops are light golden brown and a tester inserted in the center comes out clean. Let cool in pan on a wire rack for 3 minutes, then transfer to the rack to cool.

Cheese, Almond and Mushroom Muffins

These muffins are almost quiche-like and make a great filling breakfast. They are full of protein, thanks to the eggs, cottage cheese and almond flour.

Tip

Store cooled muffins in an airtight container in the refrigerator for up to 3 days.

- **12-cup muffin pan, 9 cups greased**

1 tsp	olive oil	5 mL
8 oz	cremini or button mushrooms, coarsely chopped	250 g
1 cup	almond flour	250 mL
1 tsp	baking powder	5 mL
1/4 tsp	freshly ground black pepper	1 mL
4	large eggs	4
2/3 cup	cottage cheese	150 mL
2 tbsp	freshly grated Parmesan cheese	30 mL
1/2 cup	crumbled feta cheese	125 mL
1/4 cup	chopped green onions	60 mL

1. In a large skillet, heat oil over medium-high heat. Add mushrooms and cook, stirring, for 4 to 5 minutes or until starting to brown and liquid has evaporated. Remove from heat and let cool.

2. Preheat oven to 400°F (200°C).

3. In a large bowl, whisk together flour, baking powder and pepper. Stir in eggs, cottage cheese and Parmesan until just blended. Fold in sautéed mushrooms, feta and green onions.

4. Divide batter equally among prepared muffin cups.

5. Bake for 23 to 25 minutes or until tops are golden and a tester inserted in the center comes out clean. Let cool in pan on a wire rack for 5 minutes, then transfer to the rack to cool slightly. Serve warm or let cool to room temperature.

Cocoa Quinoa Breakfast Squares

These tasty breakfast squares could almost pass for brownies, but with good-for-you ingredients for your family to start their day.

Tips

Lining a pan with foil is easy. Begin by turning the pan upside down. Tear off a piece of foil longer than the pan, then mold the foil over the pan. Remove the foil and set it aside. Flip the pan over and gently fit the shaped foil into the pan, allowing the foil to hang over the sides (the overhang ends will work as "handles" when the contents of the pan are removed).

Wrap the cooled squares in parchment or plastic wrap for a perfectly portable, make-ahead breakfast.

Store the cooled quinoa squares tightly covered or in an airtight container in the refrigerator for up to 3 days. Serve cold or at room temperature.

- Preheat oven to 350°F (180°C)
- Blender or food processor
- 8-inch (20 cm) square metal baking pan, lined with foil (see tip) and sprayed with nonstick cooking spray

1 cup	pitted soft dates (such as Medjool)	250 mL
1/3 cup	unsweetened cocoa powder	75 mL
1/4 tsp	salt	1 mL
2 cups	milk or plain non-dairy milk (such as soy, rice, almond or hemp)	500 mL
1 tsp	vanilla extract	5 mL
3 cups	hot cooked quinoa	750 mL
1/2 cup	ground flax seeds (flaxseed meal)	125 mL

1. In blender, combine dates, cocoa, salt, milk and vanilla; purée until smooth.

2. Transfer date mixture to a large bowl and stir in quinoa and flax seeds. Spread evenly in prepared pan.

3. Bake in preheated oven for 55 to 60 minutes or until firmly set. Let cool completely in pan on a wire rack. Using foil liner, lift mixture from pan onto a cutting board; peel off foil and cut into 9 squares.

Multigrain Cranberry Breakfast Cookies

Makes 2½ dozen cookies

These breakfast cookies are nice and soft, so they will be easy for your baby to grasp and eat. Experts recommend offering peanut butter to your baby a few times a week, and one option is to include it in baked goods, like these cookies.

Tip

Store cooled cookies in an airtight container in the refrigerator for up to 5 days.

- Preheat oven to 350°F (180°C)
- Baking sheets, lined with parchment paper

1 cup	rolled barley flakes or large-flake (old-fashioned) rolled oats	250 mL
½ cup	whole wheat flour	125 mL
¼ cup	instant skim milk powder	60 mL
2 tsp	ground cinnamon	10 mL
¼ tsp	baking soda	1 mL
¼ tsp	salt	1 mL
½ cup	mashed ripe banana	125 mL
½ cup	unsweetened natural peanut butter or other nut butter	125 mL
¼ cup	pure maple syrup	60 mL
1 tsp	vanilla extract	5 mL
¾ cup	dried cranberries, blueberries or cherries, chopped	175 mL

1. In a large bowl, whisk together barley, flour, milk powder, cinnamon, baking soda and salt. Stir in banana, peanut butter, maple syrup and vanilla until just blended. Gently fold in cranberries.

2. Drop batter by 2 tbsp (30 mL) onto prepared baking sheets, spacing cookies 2 inches (5 cm) apart. With a metal spatula, flatten each mound to ½-inch (1 cm) thickness.

3. Bake one sheet at a time in preheated oven for 12 to 15 minutes or until just set at the center. Let cool in pan on a wire rack for 5 minutes, then transfer to the rack to cool.

Berry Protein Shake

Adding flax seeds (or hemp or chia seeds) to your smoothies gives them extra protein as well as omega-3 fats. Soft tofu blends easily and is a good source of protein and some iron for your baby.

• **Blender**

1 cup	frozen berries (such as strawberries, blueberries, blackberries and/or raspberries)	250 mL
1 cup	sliced frozen ripe banana	250 mL
1 cup	drained soft silken tofu	250 mL
¾ cup	cold water	175 mL
1 tbsp	ground flax seeds (flaxseed meal)	15 mL

1. In blender, purée berries, banana, tofu, cold water and flax seeds until smooth. Pour into two glasses and serve immediately.

Super Antioxidant Smoothie

Makes 2 servings

Leafy spinach is difficult for toothless babies to eat and could be a choking hazard. Blending spinach into smoothies is one way to get this nutrient-dense greenery into your baby's diet!

• **Blender**

1 cup	loosely packed baby spinach	250 mL
1 cup	frozen cherries, blueberries or blackberries	250 mL
1 cup	milk	250 mL

1. In blender, purée spinach, cherries and milk until smooth. Pour into two glasses and serve immediately.

Lunches

Curried Butternut Squash and Bean Soup

This soup is thick, so it's a good starter soup when your baby is learning to use a spoon. Or serve it in a cup for baby to drink, or with a breadstick to dip!

Tip

To make 2 cups (500 mL) mashed cooked butternut squash, use 1 medium squash. Cut it in half lengthwise and scoop out the seeds. Place it cut side down on a lightly greased baking sheet and prick the skin several times with a fork. Bake in a 375°F (190°C) oven for about 30 minutes or until fork-tender. Let cool, then scoop out the flesh and discard the skin. If you have more flesh than you need, reserve the extra for another use.

- **Food processor, blender or immersion blender**

1 tbsp	canola oil	15 mL
½ cup	coarsely chopped onion	125 mL
½ cup	coarsely chopped carrot	125 mL
½ cup	coarsely chopped celery	125 mL
2	cloves garlic, minced	2
1 tsp	minced gingerroot	5 mL
2 tsp	curry powder	10 mL
1½ tsp	ground cumin	7 mL
1	can (19 oz/540 mL) white kidney beans, drained and rinsed	1
2 cups	mashed cooked butternut squash (see tip)	500 mL
2 cups	ready-to-use low-sodium vegetable broth	500 mL
2 cups	water	500 mL
	Salt and freshly ground black pepper	

1. In a large pot, heat oil over medium-high heat. Add onion, carrot and celery; cook, stirring, for 4 to 5 minutes or until softened. Add garlic, ginger, curry powder and cumin; cook, stirring, for 30 seconds. Stir in beans, squash, broth and water; bring to a boil. Reduce heat and simmer, stirring occasionally, for 30 minutes to blend the flavors.

2. Working in batches, transfer soup to food processor (or use immersion blender in pot) and purée until smooth. Return soup to pot (if necessary) and season to taste with salt and pepper.

Variation

Use acorn squash instead of butternut.

This recipe courtesy of dietitian Rosie Dhaliwal.

Sweet Potato and Bean Wraps

Makes 6 servings

Refried beans make a great spread or dip for your little one, providing iron, protein and fiber. Look for low-sodium canned refried beans.

Tip
Serve with salsa and sour cream or yogurt.

1	sweet potato	1
6	10-inch (25 cm) flour tortillas	6
1	can (14 oz/398 mL) refried beans	1
2 cups	lightly packed spinach leaves, chopped	500 mL
1	avocado, sliced	1

1. Pierce sweet potato with a fork. Microwave on High for 5 minutes or until tender. Slice lengthwise, scoop out flesh and mash in a bowl.

2. On the bottom third of each tortilla, place one-sixth of each of the sweet potato, refried beans, spinach and avocado. Fold in the 2 sides, then fold the bottom of the wrap up over the filling and roll until tight.

3. Microwave wraps on High for 45 seconds or until heated through.

This recipe courtesy of dietitians Heidi Piovoso and Kristyn Hall.

Potato and Cheese Pyrohy

These make a perfect
easy-to-grasp, soft and
mild-tasting meal for
your baby-led weaner!
Offer the sour cream so
your baby can practice
dipping them.

Tips

Pyrohy, also known as
pirozhki and pierogi, are
dumplings of Eastern
European origin. Many
cultures make a dumpling-
like food: Asian potstickers,
Japanese gyoza, Italian
ravioli and Swedish palt,
for example.

The pyrohy dough can be
left out, covered, for several
hours. It becomes softer
with resting.

The cooking time of the
pyrohy will vary depending
on their size and the
thickness of the dough.

This recipe courtesy of
dietitian Dianna Bihun.

Dough

3 cups	all-purpose flour (approx.)	750 mL
Pinch	salt	Pinch
1 tbsp	canola oil	15 mL
1½ cups	warm water	375 mL

Potato and Cheese Filling

4	baking potatoes, peeled and chopped	4
1 cup	shredded Cheddar cheese or dry-pressed cottage cheese	250 mL
2 tbsp	canola oil	30 mL
2 tbsp	finely chopped onion	30 mL
	Freshly ground black pepper (optional)	

Topping

1 tbsp	canola oil	15 mL
½ cup	finely chopped onion	125 mL
½ cup	sour cream	125 mL

1. *Dough:* In a large bowl, combine flour and salt.
   Gradually add oil, then warm water, incorporating
   flour with a wooden spoon as you pour. Stir until
   mixture holds together. Transfer to a lightly floured
   work surface and knead for about 10 minutes, until
   a soft and pliable dough forms, adding more flour as
   necessary to prevent sticking. Invert the bowl over
   the dough and let rest for at least 10 minutes.

2. *Filling:* Meanwhile, fill a large pot with water and
   bring to a boil over high heat. Add potatoes, reduce
   heat and boil gently for about 15 minutes or until
   fork-tender. Drain and transfer to another large bowl.
   Mash until fairly smooth. If using Cheddar cheese,
   stir it in now so it will melt, then let the mixture cool.

3. In a small skillet, heat oil over medium-high heat.
   Add onion and cook, stirring, for about 3 minutes
   or until softened. Stir into mashed potatoes. If using
   cottage cheese, stir it in now. Season to taste with
   salt and pepper (if using). Let cool completely.

Serving Idea

Serve alongside other traditional Eastern European foods, such as cabbage rolls.

4. Pinch off a ball of dough about the diameter of a golf ball. On a clean, lightly floured surface, roll out the dough until it is very thin (no thicker than about $1/8$ inch/3 mm) and 2 to $2^1/_2$ inches (5 to 6 cm) in diameter. Place the circle in the palm of your hand and place about 1 tsp (5 mL) filling in the center. Fold the circle in half and press the edges together with your fingers, making sure no filling has seeped through to the edges. Place pyrohy on a lightly floured board or work surface and cover with a clean tea towel. Do not let them stick together. Repeat with the remaining dough and filling.

5. In a large pot of boiling water, boil 10 to 15 pyrohy at a time, stirring gently with a wooden spoon to separate and prevent sticking, for 3 to 5 minutes or until puffed. Using a slotted spoon; transfer pyrohy to a serving dish.

6. *Topping:* Meanwhile, in a small skillet, heat oil over medium heat. Add onion and cook, stirring, for about 8 minutes or until lightly browned. Add to pyrohy and toss gently to coat. Serve with sour cream on the side.

Variations

Instead of the potato mixture, try filling each pyrohy with 1 tsp (5 mL) finely chopped sautéed mushrooms.

Fill each pyrohy with 1 tsp (5 mL) sauerkraut with sautéed onions in place of the potato filling.

Barley Terrine

Barley is a gluten-free grain. With the addition of eggs and cheese, the barley in this recipe becomes a tasty protein-rich meal or side dish.

Tip

Pot barley (also called Scotch barley) has only the outermost hull and bran removed during processing, while pearl barley also has the endosperm removed. Both are widely available for cooking. Pot barley takes about an hour to cook; pearl barley takes about 35 minutes. You can use pearl barley in this recipe if you adjust the cooking time in step 1 accordingly.

Serving Idea

Serve topped with your favorite tomato sauce, along with sautéed snow peas.

- Preheat oven to 350°F (180°C)
- 9- by 5-inch (23 by 12.5 cm) metal loaf pan, greased

1¾ cups	water	425 mL
⅔ cup	pot barley	150 mL
3	large eggs, lightly beaten	3
2 cups	shredded Cheddar cheese	500 mL
1 cup	chopped onion	250 mL
⅔ cup	finely diced celery	150 mL
½ cup	wheat germ	125 mL
⅓ cup	ground sunflower seeds	75 mL
¼ cup	finely chopped walnuts	60 mL
¼ cup	chopped fresh parsley	60 mL
½ tsp	dried thyme	2 mL
½ tsp	freshly ground black pepper	2 mL

1. In a medium saucepan, bring water to a boil over high heat. Stir in barley. Reduce heat to low, cover and simmer for 1 hour or until tender. Drain and discard any excess water. Transfer barley to a large bowl and let cool slightly.

2. Add eggs, cheese, onion, celery, wheat germ, sunflower seeds, walnuts, parsley, thyme and pepper to barley and stir to form a uniform mixture. Press gently into prepared loaf pan.

3. Bake in preheated oven for 50 minutes or until firm to the touch. Remove and let stand for 10 minutes. Unmold onto a cutting board and cut into 8 slices.

This recipe courtesy of dietitian Danielle Lamontagne.

Quinoa Vegetable Cakes

Makes 4 servings

These vegetarian patties make a tasty lunch, with yogurt for dipping. Quinoa is a rare vegetarian source of complete protein, offering all the amino acids the body needs.

- Preheat oven to 400°F (200°C)
- Large rimmed baking sheet, sprayed with nonstick cooking spray (preferably olive oil)

2	cloves garlic, minced	2
1	package (10 oz/300 g) frozen chopped spinach, thawed and squeezed dry	1
3 cups	cooked quinoa, cooled	750 mL
¾ cup	finely shredded carrots	175 mL
½ cup	finely chopped green onions	125 mL
¼ cup	whole wheat flour	60 mL
1 tbsp	dried Italian seasoning	15 mL
1 tsp	baking powder	5 mL
½ tsp	freshly ground black pepper	2 mL
1	large egg, lightly beaten	1
1 tbsp	chopped fresh dill	15 mL
1 cup	plain yogurt	250 mL
1 tbsp	freshly squeezed lemon juice	15 mL

1. In a large bowl, combine garlic, spinach, quinoa, carrots, green onions, flour, Italian seasoning, baking powder, pepper and egg.

2. Scoop 8 equal mounds of quinoa mixture onto prepared baking sheet. Flatten to ½-inch (1 cm) thickness with a spatula.

3. Bake in preheated oven for 15 minutes. Turn cakes over and bake for 8 to 12 minutes or until golden brown and hot in the center.

4. In a small bowl, whisk together dill, yogurt and lemon juice. Serve warm quinoa cakes with yogurt sauce drizzled on top or served alongside.

Lentil Patties with Herbed Yogurt Sauce

Makes 6 servings

Lentils are an inexpensive, easy-to-prepare vegetarian protein source. Legumes such as lentils are also an excellent source of fiber, great for keeping your baby regular!

Tip

Red lentils are recommended for this recipe because they cook so quickly, but if green or brown lentils are what's on hand, use either instead. Just be sure to cook them until very tender.

- **Large rimmed baking sheet, lined with foil and sprayed with nonstick cooking spray**

1½ cups	dried red lentils, rinsed	375 mL
4 cups	water	1 L
1 tbsp	extra virgin olive oil	15 mL
1 cup	finely chopped onion	250 mL
1½ cups	finely shredded carrots	375 mL
3	cloves garlic, minced	3
1½ tsp	ground cumin	7 mL
¼ tsp	salt	1 mL
⅛ tsp	cayenne pepper	0.5 mL
¾ cup	fresh whole wheat bread crumbs	175 mL
¾ cup	packed fresh flat-leaf (Italian) parsley leaves, divided	175 mL
2	large eggs, lightly beaten	2
	Nonstick cooking spray	
1 cup	plain yogurt	250 mL
1 tbsp	freshly squeezed lemon juice	15 mL

1. In a medium saucepan, combine lentils and water. Bring to a boil over medium-high heat. Reduce heat and simmer for about 22 minutes or until very tender but not mushy. Drain and let cool completely.

2. Preheat broiler, with rack set 4 to 6 inches (10 to 15 cm) from the heat source.

3. In a large skillet, heat oil over medium-high heat. Add onion and cook, stirring, for 5 to 6 minutes or until softened. Add carrots and cook, stirring, for 2 to 3 minutes or until softened. Add garlic, cumin, salt and cayenne; cook, stirring, for 30 seconds.

Tip

The patties can be prepared through step 4, covered and refrigerated overnight.

4. In a large bowl, combine cooled lentils, onion mixture, bread crumbs, half the parsley and eggs. Shape into 12 balls. Place balls on prepared baking sheet and flatten with a spatula to about $\frac{1}{2}$-inch (1 cm) thickness. Spray tops with cooking spray.

5. Broil patties, turning once, for 3 to 4 minutes per side or until golden brown on both sides and hot in the center.

6. Meanwhile, in a small bowl, whisk together the remaining parsley, yogurt and lemon juice. Serve lentil patties drizzled with yogurt sauce.

Best Black Bean Burgers

Makes 4 servings

To feed your baby this family-friendly meal, offer her the plain bean burger patty with the yogurt for dipping.

Tip

If you can only find larger 19-oz (540 mL) cans of beans, you will need about 1½ cans (3 cups/750 mL drained).

- **Food processor**

1	slice whole-grain bread	1
2	cans (each 14 to 15 oz/398 to 425 mL) black beans, drained and rinsed, divided	2
1	large egg	1
¼ cup	finely chopped fresh cilantro	60 mL
2 tsp	ground cumin	10 mL
1 tsp	dried oregano	5 mL
¼ tsp	cayenne pepper	1 mL
1 tbsp	extra virgin olive oil	15 mL
4	whole wheat hamburger buns, split and toasted	4

Suggested Accompaniments

Plain Greek yogurt

Salsa

Spinach leaves

1. In food processor, pulse bread into crumbs. Add half the beans, egg, cilantro, cumin, oregano and cayenne; pulse until a chunky purée forms.

2. Transfer purée to a medium bowl and stir in the remaining beans. Form into four ¾-inch (2 cm) thick patties.

3. In a large skillet, heat oil over medium heat. Add patties and cook for 4 minutes. Turn and cook for 3 to 4 minutes or until crispy on the outside and hot in the center.

4. Transfer patties to toasted buns. Top with any of the suggested accompaniments, as desired.

Variation

For vegan burgers, use 3 tbsp (45 mL) vegan mayonnaise alternative in place of the egg.

Creamed Salmon on English Muffins

Makes 4 servings

Canned fish is a good starter food for your baby. Salmon provides protein and heme iron, and is one of the best sources of the omega-3 fat DHA, which is important for your baby's brain development.

Tip

Much of the sodium in this recipe comes from the English muffins and the canned salmon. To reduce the sodium, serve the salmon mixture over steamed brown rice. Using 1¼ cups (300 mL) leftover cooked flaked salmon instead of canned will also help.

1	can (7½ oz/213 g) salmon	1
2 tsp	canola oil	10 mL
1 tbsp	finely chopped shallots	15 mL
1 tbsp	thinly sliced green onions	15 mL
2 tsp	all-purpose flour	10 mL
¼ tsp	freshly ground black pepper	1 mL
1 cup	evaporated milk	250 mL
¼ cup	thawed frozen green peas	60 mL
1 tsp	minced fresh dill	5 mL
2	whole wheat English muffins, split and toasted	2

1. Drain liquid from salmon, reserving liquid. Transfer salmon to a bowl and flake with a fork. Set both aside.

2. In a large nonstick skillet, heat oil over medium-high heat. Add shallots and green onions; cook, stirring, for about 1 minute or until softened. Reduce heat to medium and add flour and pepper; cook, stirring, for 1 minute, making sure flour does not burn.

3. Gradually stir in milk and reserved liquid from salmon, stirring until smooth. Reduce heat to low and stir in salmon and peas; simmer until heated through. Stir in dill.

4. Place toasted English muffin halves on serving plates and spoon salmon mixture over top.

Variation
Use canned tuna instead of salmon.

This recipe courtesy of Debra Palfreyman.

Balsamic Tuna Salad in Avocado Halves

Your baby will have a blast digging in to this nutritious and tasty lunch — and you'll love it too. Get the bib ready!

1	can (6 oz/170 g) tuna packed in olive oil, with oil	1
1 tsp	balsamic vinegar	5 mL
¼ tsp	Dijon mustard	1 mL
1	firm-ripe Hass avocado, peeled, halved and pitted	1

1. Drain tuna, reserving 2 tsp (10 mL) oil. In a small bowl, whisk together the reserved oil, vinegar and mustard. Set aside 1 tsp (5 mL) of the dressing. Add tuna to the remaining dressing, tossing gently to combine.

2. Fill avocado halves with tuna mixture. Drizzle with the reserved dressing.

Sautéed Peppers and Eggs

Eggs make a quick meal and supply gold-star protein for the whole family. You can offer your baby the whole egg (both yolk and white) any time after 6 months of age.

Tip
Cooking the peppers covered over a low heat draws out their moisture and flavor. The key is to make sure they don't brown.

This recipe courtesy of dietitian Francy Pillo-Blocka.

2 tsp	olive oil	10 mL
2	red bell peppers, sliced into thin strips	2
4	large eggs	4
Pinch	salt	Pinch
	Freshly ground black pepper	
2	multigrain buns, split and toasted	2

1. In a large skillet, heat oil over medium-low heat. Spread red peppers evenly in pan, cover and simmer, stirring occasionally, for 15 to 20 minutes or until peppers are very tender, but not browned. (If peppers start turning brown, add 1 to 2 tbsp/15 to 30 mL water and cover again.)

2. In a small bowl, whisk together eggs, salt and pepper to taste. Stir into skillet, cover and cook, stirring occasionally, for 2 to 3 minutes or until eggs are just set.

3. Place toasted multigrain bun halves on serving plates and spoon egg mixture over top.

Egg and Lentil Curry

Makes 4 servings

Your baby's absorption of the non-heme iron from the eggs and lentils in this recipe will be naturally increased thanks to the vitamin C in the tomatoes!

Tips

To toast cumin seeds: Place seeds in a dry skillet over medium heat, stirring, until fragrant, about 3 minutes. Immediately transfer to a mortar or a spice grinder and grind. You can substitute 1 tsp (5 mL) ground cumin for the cumin seeds, if you prefer.

This dish can be partially prepared before it is cooked. Complete step 1. Cover and refrigerate for up to 2 days. When you're ready to cook, continue with the recipe.

• **Medium to large (3½- to 6-quart) slow cooker**

1 tbsp	vegetable oil	15 mL
1½ cups	finely chopped onions	375 mL
1 tbsp	minced garlic	15 mL
1 tbsp	minced gingerroot	15 mL
1 tsp	ground coriander	5 mL
1 tsp	cumin seeds, toasted and ground (see tip)	5 mL
1 tsp	cracked black peppercorns	5 mL
1 cup	dried red lentils, rinsed	250 mL
1	can (28 oz/796 mL) no-salt-added tomatoes, including juice, coarsely chopped	1
2 cups	ready-to-use low-sodium vegetable broth	500 mL
1 cup	coconut milk	250 mL
4	hard-cooked eggs, peeled and cut in half	4
	Finely chopped parsley (optional)	

1. In a medium skillet, heat oil over medium heat for 30 seconds. Add onions and cook, stirring, until softened, about 3 minutes. Add garlic, ginger, coriander, toasted cumin and peppercorns; cook, stirring, for 1 minute. Add lentils, tomatoes and broth; bring to a boil. Transfer to slow cooker.

2. Cover and cook on Low for 8 hours or on High for 4 hours, until lentils are tender and mixture is bubbly. Stir in coconut milk, cover and cook for 20 to 30 minutes, until heated through.

3. When ready to serve, ladle into soup bowls and top each serving with 2 egg halves. Garnish with parsley (if using).

Variation

If the adults or older children in the house prefer poached eggs, you can substitute them for the hard-cooked eggs in this recipe. Poached eggs contain a slightly higher risk of carrying salmonella; it's safer to offer your baby only fully cooked eggs.

Red Lentil Frittata

Red lentils are quick to cook, soft and high in iron, protein and fiber. Mixing them with roasted red peppers, cilantro and goat cheese produces a tasty combo the whole family will love!

- 9-inch (23 cm) glass baking dish, sprayed with nonstick cooking spray (preferably olive oil)

½ cup	dried red lentils, rinsed	125 mL
2 cups	water	500 mL
8	large eggs	8
1	clove garlic, minced	1
1½ tsp	ground cumin	7 mL
¼ tsp	salt	1 mL
¼ tsp	freshly cracked black pepper	1 mL
1 cup	chopped drained roasted red bell peppers	250 mL
½ cup	packed fresh cilantro leaves, chopped	125 mL
2 oz	soft goat cheese, crumbled	60 g

1. In a medium saucepan, combine lentils and water. Bring to a boil over medium-high heat. Reduce heat and simmer for about 22 minutes or until very tender but not mushy. Drain and let cool slightly.

2. Preheat oven to 375°F (190°C).

3. In a large bowl, whisk together eggs, garlic, cumin, salt and pepper. Stir in cooked lentils, roasted peppers, cilantro and cheese. Spread evenly in prepared baking dish.

4. Bake in preheated oven for 25 to 30 minutes or until golden brown, puffed and set at the center. Let cool on a wire rack for at least 10 minutes before cutting. Serve warm or let cool completely.

Scrambled Egg Pizza

Scrambled eggs and kidney beans make the perfect protein- and iron-rich soft finger food for your baby once he has developed a pincer grasp.

Tips

If you don't have salsa on hand, you can use low-sodium pasta sauce.

For the vegetables, try mushrooms, bell peppers, onions, tomatoes, asparagus and/or zucchini in your favorite combination.

- **Preheat broiler**
- **Baking sheet, lightly greased**

1	10-inch (25 cm) whole wheat flour tortilla	1
2 tbsp	drained rinsed canned kidney beans, mashed	30 mL
2 tbsp	salsa	30 mL
1 tsp	canola oil	5 mL
½ cup	chopped vegetables (see tip)	125 mL
3	large eggs	3
1 tbsp	milk	15 mL
¼ tsp	freshly ground black pepper	1 mL
¼ cup	shredded Cheddar cheese	60 mL

1. Place tortilla on prepared baking sheet. In a small bowl, combine mashed beans and salsa. Spread over tortilla and set aside.

2. In a medium nonstick skillet, heat oil over medium heat. Add vegetables and cook, stirring, for 3 to 5 minutes or until softened.

3. In a small bowl, whisk together eggs and milk. Season with pepper. Pour over vegetable mixture and cook, stirring occasionally, for about 1 minute or until eggs form soft, thick curds.

4. Spread cooked eggs evenly over tortilla and sprinkle with cheese. Broil for 1 minute or until cheese melts. Cut tortilla into quarters and serve.

This recipe courtesy of Justyne Tirrell-Kanji.

Spinach and Pesto Crustless Quiche

This flavorful quiche is a great way to offer spinach to your baby. Spinach is a nutritional powerhouse; among other things, it's a great source of folate.

Tip

If there are any leftovers, this quiche reheats well in the microwave.

Serving Idea

Serve fresh fruit and whole wheat toast alongside this quiche.

- Preheat oven to 350°F (180°C)
- 9-inch (23 cm) glass pie plate, lightly greased

5	large eggs	5
½ cup	evaporated milk	125 mL
1 tbsp	basil pesto	15 mL
1	package (10 oz/300 g) frozen spinach, thawed, drained and squeezed dry	1
1 cup	shredded mozzarella cheese	250 mL
½ cup	crumbled feta cheese	125 mL

1. In a medium bowl, whisk together eggs, evaporated milk and pesto. Stir in spinach, mozzarella and feta. Transfer to prepared baking dish.

2. Bake in preheated oven for 25 to 30 minutes or until center is firm. Let rest for 5 minutes before serving.

This recipe courtesy of Daphna Gale.

Crustless Mini Quinoa Quiches

Makes 2 dozen mini quiches

These tasty, mini-fist-friendly quiches are great to keep in the freezer and defrost for a quick meal or even a balanced snack.

Tip

Larger quiches can be made by using a 12-cup regular muffin pan. Bake for 23 to 28 minutes.

- Preheat oven to 350°F (180°C)
- Blender or food processor
- Two 12-cup mini muffin pans, sprayed with nonstick cooking spray

2	cloves garlic, roughly chopped	2
1/8 tsp	freshly ground black pepper	0.5 mL
4	large eggs	4
1 cup	cottage cheese	250 mL
1 cup	cooked quinoa, cooled	250 mL
2/3 cup	drained roasted red bell peppers, chopped	150 mL
1/4 cup	packed fresh basil leaves, chopped	60 mL
1/4 cup	freshly grated Parmesan cheese	60 mL

1. In blender, combine garlic, pepper, eggs and cottage cheese; purée until smooth.

2. Transfer purée to a medium bowl and stir in quinoa, roasted peppers, basil and Parmesan.

3. Divide quinoa mixture equally among prepared muffin cups.

4. Bake in preheated oven for 18 to 23 minutes or until tops are golden brown. Let cool in pan on a wire rack for 5 minutes. Run a knife around each quiche and gently lift out of pan, then transfer to the rack to cool. Serve warm or let cool completely.

Cornmeal Crêpes with Avocado Filling

Makes 4 to 6 crêpes

Crêpes are a traditional French food. Introducing babies to flavors from around the world when they are starting solids may help them become more adventurous eaters when they are bit older!

Tips

Select an avocado that is firm to the touch yet yields with gentle pressure.

If the batter is too thick to spread, add another 1 tbsp (15 mL) milk.

If you find you cannot swirl the batter quickly enough for it to reach the edges of the pan, simply use more batter.

• 6-inch (15 cm) crêpe pan or nonstick skillet

Cornmeal Crêpes

½ cup	all-purpose flour	125 mL
⅓ cup	cornmeal	75 mL
1 tsp	baking powder	5 mL
1 tsp	granulated sugar	5 mL
¼ tsp	salt	1 mL
2	large eggs	2
1 cup	plain yogurt	250 mL
3 tbsp	milk	45 mL
2 tbsp	melted butter or non-hydrogenated margarine	30 mL
	Nonstick cooking spray	

Avocado Filling

1	large ripe avocado	1
2 tsp	freshly squeezed lemon or lime juice	10 mL
2	ripe tomatoes, seeded and finely chopped	2
½ cup	chopped green onions	125 mL
1 tsp	chile and garlic sauce	5 mL
¼ tsp	salt	1 mL
¼ tsp	freshly ground black pepper	1 mL
¼ cup	sour cream (optional)	60 mL

1. *Crêpes:* In a large bowl, combine flour, cornmeal, baking powder, sugar and salt.

2. In another large bowl, whisk together eggs, yogurt, milk and butter. Make a well in the center of the flour mixture and gradually add the egg mixture, whisking until batter is blended and smooth. Cover and let rest at room temperature for 10 minutes.

This recipe courtesy of Laura Glenn.

Nutrition Tip

Avocados are one of the few fruits that contain a substantial amount of fat. But unlike coconut (the fruit of the tropical palm tree), which contains mostly saturated fat, avocados provide mainly monounsaturated fat.

3. Heat crêpe pan over medium heat. Spray lightly with cooking spray. Lift the pan and pour in about $1/3$ cup (75 mL) batter. Swirl the pan so the batter reaches the edges. Return to heat and cook for about 1 minute or until crêpe is no longer shiny on top and is very light golden on the bottom. Flip and cook for 30 to 60 seconds or until starting to turn golden. Transfer to a plate, cover with foil and keep warm. Repeat with the remaining batter, spraying pan and adjusting heat between batches as needed.

4. *Filling:* In a small bowl, mash avocado. Sprinkle with lemon juice. Gently stir in tomatoes, green onions, chile and garlic sauce, salt and pepper.

5. Divide filling among crêpes. Fold bottom edge of crêpe over filling, then fold top edge over bottom edge. Transfer to a serving plate, seam side down. Serve with a dollop of sour cream, if desired.

Variation

Fill these crêpes with black beans, salsa and cheese in place of the avocado filling.

Pork, Apple and Sage Patties

Makes 12 patties

Pork naturally goes well with the sweet taste of apples and dried apricots in this recipe.

Tips

Be sure to turn the patties over while they're baking so that each side can brown.

These patties freeze well. Let cooked patties cool, wrap in plastic wrap, then freeze in an airtight container or freezer bag for up to 3 months. Let thaw in the refrigerator overnight and reheat before serving.

Serving Idea

Serve with your favorite pancakes, waffles or scrambled eggs.

- **Preheat oven to 375°F (190°C)**
- **Rimmed baking sheet, greased**

1 tsp	canola oil	5 mL
12 oz	lean ground pork	375 g
¾ cup	finely chopped onions	175 mL
½ cup	finely chopped peeled apple	125 mL
1	slice raisin or whole wheat bread, torn into small pieces	1
1	large egg, lightly beaten	1
¼ cup	finely diced dried apricots	60 mL
1 tbsp	pure maple syrup	15 mL
½ tsp	dried savory	2 mL
½ tsp	dried marjoram	2 mL
1 tsp	ground sage	5 mL
¼ tsp	salt	1 mL

1. In a large nonstick skillet, heat oil over medium heat. Add pork and cook, breaking it up with a spoon, for about 8 minutes or until no longer pink. Add onions and apple; cook, stirring, for about 5 minutes or until softened.

2. Transfer pork mixture to a large bowl and stir in bread, egg, apricots, maple syrup, savory, marjoram, sage and salt. Using about ¼ cup (60 mL) mixture, form into ½-inch (1 cm) thick patties and place about 2 inches (5 cm) apart on prepared baking sheet.

3. Bake in preheated oven, turning once, for 15 to 20 minutes or until an instant-read thermometer inserted horizontally into the center of a patty registers 160°F (71°C).

Variation

Use raisins, dried cherries or blueberries instead of the apricots.

This recipe courtesy of dietitian Mary Sue Waisman.

Beef, Vegetable and Bean Soup

Makes 8 servings

This recipe is good practice for your baby's pincer grasp. Pick out the soft pieces of meat, vegetable and pasta from the soup and place them on your baby's tray.

Tips

If you don't have any zucchini, substitute an equal amount of frozen peas, green beans or corn.

Any 19-oz (540 mL) can of beans can be used in place of the mixed beans. Try kidney, romano or white pea beans.

This soup keeps for up to 3 days in the refrigerator or 4 months in the freezer.

12 oz	lean ground beef	375 g
2 tsp	minced garlic	10 mL
½ cup	chopped onions	125 mL
1 cup	chopped carrots	250 mL
1 cup	chopped celery or fennel	250 mL
1 cup	chopped zucchini	250 mL
1 tsp	dried basil	5 mL
1	bay leaf	1
6 cups	ready-to-use low-sodium beef broth	1.5 L
1	can (28 oz/796 mL) no-salt-added whole tomatoes	1
½ cup	macaroni (or any other small pasta)	125 mL
3 cups	fresh chopped spinach	750 mL
1	can (19 oz/540 mL) mixed beans, drained and rinsed	1

1. In a large saucepan or Dutch oven, brown beef over medium-high heat. Add garlic, onions, carrots, celery and zucchini; cook for 5 minutes. Add basil, bay leaf, broth and tomatoes; bring to a boil. Reduce heat and simmer, covered, for 10 minutes.

2. Add pasta; cook for another 5 to 6 minutes. Add spinach and beans; cook for another 3 to 4 minutes. Remove bay leaf before serving.

Hamburger Pizza Buns

Makes about 48 pizza buns

These pizza buns are a unique way to serve homemade pizza! The buns are soft and easy to grasp, and are fun to dip into extra tomato sauce.

Tips

Be sure to remove the vegetables from the heat before adding the cheese, so the cheese doesn't melt.

This recipe works well halved, for a smaller crowd.

Use your imagination for the fillings. Try cooked broccoli and shredded cheese, or pesto and cooked chicken, in place of the ground beef mixture.

This recipe courtesy of dietitian Lindsay McGregor.

- Baking sheets, lightly greased

Bun Dough

½ cup	granulated sugar	125 mL
2 tbsp	quick-rising (instant) yeast	30 mL
1 tsp	salt	5 mL
2	large eggs, beaten	2
3 cups	warm water	750 mL
¼ cup	canola oil	60 mL
5 cups	whole wheat flour	1.25 L
4 cups	all-purpose flour	1 L

Filling

2 lb	lean ground beef	1 kg
2 cups	finely chopped mushrooms	500 mL
1½ cups	finely chopped onions	375 mL
1 cup	finely chopped green bell pepper	250 mL
1	can (14 oz/398 mL) low-sodium tomato sauce	1
3 cups	shredded Cheddar cheese	750 mL
1 tbsp	dried oregano	15 mL
	Freshly ground black pepper	

1. *Dough:* In a large bowl, combine sugar, yeast, salt, eggs, warm water and oil. Gradually stir in whole wheat flour and all-purpose flour until incorporated.

2. Turn dough out onto a floured surface and knead for about 5 minutes or until smooth. Place in lightly greased large bowl, cover with plastic wrap and let rise in a warm, draft-free place for about 45 minutes or until doubled in bulk. Punch dough down, cover and let rise again for about 45 minutes or until doubled in bulk. Meanwhile, preheat oven to 350°F (180°C).

3. *Filling:* Meanwhile, in a large skillet over medium-high heat, cook beef, breaking it up with the back of a spoon, for about 8 minutes or until no longer pink. Using a slotted spoon, transfer beef to a bowl. Drain off all but 2 tsp (10 mL) fat from the pan.

4. Reduce heat to medium. Add mushrooms, onions and green pepper to the skillet and cook, stirring, for 4 to 5 minutes or until softened. Remove from heat and stir in reserved beef, tomato sauce, cheese, oregano and pepper to taste.

5. Punch dough down. Pinch off a piece of dough about the size of a golf ball and roll it out on a floured surface to a 3- to $3\frac{1}{2}$-inch (7.5 to 9 cm) circle. Place about $1\frac{1}{2}$ tbsp (22 mL) filling in center of dough, wrap dough around filling and firmly pinch edges together to seal. Place seam side down on a prepared baking sheet (do not let rise). Repeat with the remaining dough and filling, placing buns about 2 inches (5 cm) apart.

6. Bake one sheet at a time in preheated oven for 20 to 25 minutes or until buns are lightly browned.

Eben's Special Meatballs

**Makes
21 meatballs**

Meatballs are a favorite in my house! They're a great finger-friendly way to cook ground beef, which is one of the best sources of iron for your baby.

Tip

Make these meatballs on the weekend, then warm them up when your kids come home for lunch for "Meatball Monday."

Serving Idea

Serve with a whole-grain bun, cucumber slices and carrot sticks.

- **Preheat oven to 350°F (180°C)**
- **Rimmed baking sheet, lined with parchment paper**

1 lb	extra-lean ground beef	500 g
1	large egg, beaten	1
1 cup	finely chopped onion	250 mL
1 cup	shredded sharp (old) Cheddar cheese	250 mL
1 tbsp	Worcestershire sauce	15 mL
½ tsp	freshly ground black pepper	2 mL

Dipping Sauce

½ cup	ketchup	125 mL
¼ cup	prepared yellow mustard	60 mL

1. In a large bowl, combine beef, egg, onion, cheese, Worcestershire sauce and pepper. Shape into $1\frac{1}{2}$-inch (4 cm) round meatballs and place at least 1 inch (2.5 cm) apart on prepared baking sheet.

2. Bake in preheated oven for 25 to 30 minutes or until no longer pink inside.

3. *Sauce:* In a small bowl, combine ketchup and mustard. Divide among individual serving bowls and serve with meatballs for dipping.

This recipe courtesy of Eben Thorpe-Keith.

Dinners

Spinach Tortilla Pie

Makes 6 servings

This layered tortilla, egg and cheese dish is easy to eat and nutritious for beginning baby-led weaners. Cut the pie into thin wedges that your baby can grasp.

Tip

Although nutmeg that is purchased ground retains fragrance, flavor and taste better than some other spices, for this recipe, using whole nutmeg and grating it fresh will give you the full impact of this warm, aromatic spice. Grind it using a special nutmeg grater, or use the finest blade of a box grater. If you use purchased ground nutmeg instead, reduce the amount by half. Freshly grated is fluffier and takes up less volume to get the same flavor.

Serving Idea

Add roasted vegetables for a delicious dinner.

- **Preheat oven to 350°F (180°C)**
- **9-inch (23 cm) deep-dish glass pie plate, greased**

1 tsp	vegetable oil	5 mL
1	onion, chopped	1
1	package (10 oz/300 g) baby spinach, chopped	1
3	large eggs, beaten	3
2 cups	ricotta cheese	500 mL
½ tsp	freshly grated nutmeg (see tip)	2 mL
½ tsp	freshly ground black pepper	2 mL
3	6-inch (15 cm) whole wheat flour tortillas	3
⅓ cup	freshly grated Parmesan cheese	75 mL

1. In a medium skillet, heat oil over medium-high heat. Add onion and cook, stirring, until lightly browned, about 5 minutes. Add spinach, cover and steam, stirring occasionally to prevent burning, until wilted, about 3 minutes. Transfer mixture to a colander to remove any liquid.

2. In a medium bowl, combine spinach mixture, eggs, ricotta cheese, nutmeg and pepper.

3. Place 1 tortilla in prepared pie plate. Top with one-third of the spinach and egg mixture. Repeat twice, ending with filling on top. Sprinkle with Parmesan cheese.

4. Bake in preheated oven for 40 to 45 minutes or until eggs are set, top is lightly browned and puffed and a knife inserted in the center comes out clean.

This recipe courtesy of Maureen Falkine.

Lentils Bolognese

This is a great vegetarian option for a pasta topping. Serve with rotini, which is easy for your baby to grasp.

Serving Idea
Serve on top of whole wheat spaghetti and sprinkle with freshly grated Parmesan cheese.

1 cup	dried brown or red lentils, rinsed	250 mL
2 cups	water	500 mL
1	bay leaf	1
2 tbsp	olive oil	30 mL
2	cloves garlic, crushed	2
1	onion, finely chopped	1
1 cup	sliced mushrooms	250 mL
1 cup	chopped canned low-sodium tomatoes	250 mL
1	can (5½ oz/156 mL) tomato paste	1
1	apple, peeled and diced	1
½ cup	apple cider vinegar	125 mL
1 tsp	dried oregano	5 mL
	Juice of 1 lemon	

1. In a medium saucepan, bring lentils, water and bay leaf to a boil over high heat. Reduce heat to medium and cook for about 20 minutes or until lentils are soft. Drain and rinse and discard bay leaf. Set aside.

2. In a large saucepan, heat oil over medium heat. Add garlic, onion and mushrooms; cook, stirring, until softened, about 5 minutes. Add cooked lentils, tomatoes, tomato paste, apple, vinegar, oregano and lemon juice; bring to a boil. Reduce heat, cover and simmer for 45 minutes.

This recipe courtesy of Elaine Bass.

Lentil Shepherd's Pie

| | **Makes 4 servings** | |

This dish makes for a fun, messy finger food. Dress your baby in a full-body bib or no clothing at all — or plan for an after-dinner bath!

Tips

Use shredded Cheddar cheese instead of the Italian 4-cheese mixture, if you prefer.

Substitute ½ cup (125 mL) loosely packed parsley leaves for the green onions, if you prefer.

Be careful not to overprocess the potato mixture or the topping will be mushy. Small lumps of potato should remain.

- Preheat oven to 350°F (180°C)
- Food processor
- 8-cup (2 L) baking dish, lightly greased

Topping

1	can (19 oz/540 mL) potatoes, drained, or 2 cups (500 mL) cubed cooked potatoes	1
½ cup	milk	125 mL
1 cup	shredded Italian 4-cheese mix	250 mL
½ cup	dry bread crumbs	125 mL
4	green onions (white part only), coarsely chopped	4
1 tbsp	butter, softened	15 mL
	Freshly ground black pepper	

Filling

1 tbsp	vegetable oil	15 mL
2 cups	finely chopped onions	500 mL
1 cup	diced celery	250 mL
1	can (28 oz/796 mL) no-salt-added tomatoes, drained and coarsely chopped	1
1	can (19 oz/540 mL) lentils, drained and rinsed	1
2 tbsp	basil pesto	30 mL
2 tbsp	shredded Italian 4-cheese mix	30 mL

1. *Topping:* In food processor, combine potatoes and milk. Pulse several times to combine. Add cheese, bread crumbs, onions, butter and black pepper to taste. Process until blended but potatoes are still a bit lumpy. Set aside.

2. *Filling:* In a skillet, heat oil over medium heat. Add onion and celery; cook, stirring, until celery is softened, about 8 minutes. Add tomatoes and lentils; bring to a boil. Stir in pesto and pour into prepared baking dish.

3. Spread reserved potato mixture evenly over lentil mixture. Sprinkle with shredded cheese. Bake in preheated oven until top is browned and mixture is bubbling, about 25 minutes.

Sweet Potatoes and Carrots with Chickpea Topping

Makes 4 servings

Your baby will enjoy this slightly sweet-tasting dish, which is full of beta-carotene from the carrots and sweet potatoes.

Tips

This dish can be partially prepared the night before it is cooked. Complete steps 1 and 2. Cover and refrigerate overnight. The next morning, continue with the recipe.

Refrigerate any leftovers and transform them into an interesting side dish. Simply purée in a food processor, then reheat in the microwave or over low heat on the stovetop.

- **Large (minimum 5-quart) slow cooker, greased**
- **Food processor**

2	sweet potatoes (each about 8 oz/250 g), peeled and cut into ½-inch (1 cm) cubes	2
6	carrots, peeled and thinly sliced	6
1	can (14 oz/398 mL) crushed pineapple, drained, ¼ cup (60 mL) juice reserved	1
2 tbsp	packed brown sugar	30 mL

Topping

2 cups	cooked dried or canned chickpeas, drained and rinsed	500 mL
1 tbsp	minced garlic	15 mL
½ cup	ready-to-use low-sodium vegetable broth	125 mL
	Salt and freshly ground black pepper	

1. In prepared slow cooker, combine sweet potato, carrots and pineapple. In a small bowl, combine brown sugar and reserved pineapple juice. Add to slow cooker and stir to blend.

2. *Topping:* In food processor, process chickpeas, garlic and broth until mixture is well combined but chickpeas are still a little chunky. Season to taste with salt and pepper. Spread mixture evenly over sweet potato mixture.

3. Cover and cook on Low for 8 hours or on High for 4 hours until vegetables are tender.

Spinach and Black Bean Pasta

Broccoli and pasta offer
your baby easy-to-grasp
choices for the beginning
palmer grasp, and black
beans to practice the
pincer grasp.

Tips

This recipe can easily be
cut in half.

Older siblings will love to
"taste test" cooking pasta
for doneness.

Leftovers are delicious
placed in individual
casseroles or ramekins,
topped with cheese
and broiled.

1 lb	whole wheat rotini or penne pasta	500 g
1 tbsp	canola oil	15 mL
1 cup	chopped onion	250 mL
1	clove garlic, minced	1
1 tsp	dried oregano	5 mL
1 tsp	ground cumin	5 mL
½ tsp	freshly ground black pepper	2 mL
¼ tsp	cayenne pepper	1 mL
1	can (28 oz/796 mL) low-sodium diced tomatoes, with juice	1
1	can (5½ oz/156 mL) low-sodium tomato paste	1
1	can (19 oz/540 mL) black beans, drained and rinsed	1
1	bag (10 oz/300 g) fresh spinach, trimmed and torn into bite-size pieces	1
2 cups	chopped broccoli	500 mL
1¼ cups	ready-to-use low-sodium vegetable broth	300 mL
1 cup	water	250 mL
½ cup	freshly grated Parmesan cheese	125 mL

1. In a large pot of boiling water, cook pasta for 6 to
   8 minutes or until almost al dente. Drain and set aside.

2. Meanwhile, in a large skillet, heat oil over medium
   heat. Add onion and cook, stirring, for 3 to 4 minutes
   or until softened. Add garlic, oregano, cumin, black
   pepper and cayenne; cook, stirring, for 1 minute. Stir
   in tomatoes, tomato paste, beans, spinach, broccoli,
   broth and water; bring to a boil. Reduce heat to low
   and simmer, stirring occasionally, for 7 to 8 minutes
   or until broccoli is tender.

3. Gently stir in pasta and Parmesan; simmer for
   5 minutes or until pasta is al dente.

This recipe courtesy of
Sarah Reid.

Butternut Chili

Chili is a great dish to double and keep in the freezer for busy nights, so you can avoid takeout.

Tip

This dish can be partially prepared before it is cooked. Complete step 1, let cool, transfer to an airtight container and refrigerate overnight. The next morning, continue with the recipe.

• **Large (minimum 5-quart) slow cooker**

1 tbsp	vegetable oil	15 mL
1 lb	lean ground beef	500 g
2	onions, finely chopped	2
4	cloves garlic, minced	4
1 tbsp	cumin seeds, toasted and ground (see tip, page 145)	15 mL
2 tsp	dried oregano	10 mL
½ tsp	cracked black peppercorns	2 mL
1	2-inch (5 cm) cinnamon stick	1
1	can (28 oz/796 mL) no-salt-added diced tomatoes, with juice	1
3 cups	cubed peeled butternut squash (1-inch/2.5 cm cubes)	750 mL
2 cups	cooked dried or canned kidney beans, drained and rinsed	500 mL
½ cup	finely chopped fresh cilantro	125 mL

1. In a large skillet, heat oil over medium-high heat for 30 seconds. Add beef and onions; cook, stirring, until beef is no longer pink, about 5 minutes. Add garlic, toasted cumin, oregano, peppercorns and cinnamon stick; cook, stirring, for 1 minute. Add tomatoes and bring to a boil.

2. Place squash and beans in slow cooker and cover with sauce. Cover and cook on Low for 6 to 8 hours or on High for 3 to 4 hours, until squash is tender. Stir in cilantro.

Tofu and Spinach Lasagna

Makes 6 servings

This vegetarian lasagna is easy to make and delicious. Let your baby experiment with using a plastic fork to dig in — she will be able to maneuver a fork before she masters scooping with a spoon.

Tips

To thaw spinach quickly, heat a skillet over medium heat and add frozen spinach block. Heat, turning often, until thawed. Transfer to a colander and drain off excess water.

Leftovers of this lasagna freeze well. Wrap cooled lasagna in plastic wrap and place in an airtight container or freezer bag.

- **Preheat oven to 350°F (180°C)**
- **13- by 9-inch (33 by 23 cm) baking dish**

1 tbsp	canola oil	15 mL
1	small onion, finely chopped	1
1	carrot, finely diced	1
1	package (18 oz/540 g) soft tofu, drained	1
1	package (10 oz/300 g) frozen chopped spinach, thawed and drained	1
1	large egg, lightly beaten	1
1/3 cup	fine dry bread crumbs	75 mL
2/3 cup	water, divided	150 mL
1	jar (22 oz/650 mL) low-sodium tomato and basil pasta sauce	1
12	oven-ready lasagna noodles	12
1 cup	shredded Cheddar cheese	250 mL

1. In a large nonstick skillet, heat oil over medium-high heat. Add onion and carrot; cook, stirring, for 4 to 5 minutes or until softened.

2. Meanwhile, in a large bowl, mash tofu with a fork. Stir in onion mixture and spinach. Add egg and bread crumbs; mix well.

3. Pour 1/3 cup (75 mL) water into the baking dish, along with one-third of the pasta sauce. Mix together and spread over bottom of dish. Add the remaining water to the pasta sauce remaining in the jar and mix well.

This recipe courtesy of dietitian Caroline Dubeau.

Nutrition Tip

Many purchased pasta sauces are high in sodium. Look for ones that are labeled "lower in salt," "lower in sodium" or "no salt added" and select one that contains the least amount of sodium per serving.

Serving Idea

Serve with steamed asparagus.

4. Arrange 3 lasagna noodles on top of sauce in dish. Spread half the tofu mixture over noodles. Top with 3 lasagna noodles and pour half the remaining pasta sauce evenly over noodles. Top with 3 noodles and spread with the remaining tofu mixture. Top with the remaining 3 noodles and pour the remaining sauce over top. Sprinkle with cheese and cover with foil.

5. Bake in preheated oven for 45 to 50 minutes or until sauce is bubbling. Remove foil and bake for 10 minutes or until noodles are tender and top is browned. Let stand for 10 minutes before cutting.

Variations

When bell peppers are in season, replace the carrot with 1 finely chopped red or orange bell pepper.

Try using herb-and-garlic-flavored tofu.

Look for oven-ready whole wheat lasagna noodles to use instead of white.

Butternut Squash, Spinach and Feta Frittata

Makes 12 servings

Not only are eggs high in some hard-to-find nutrients, such as choline, but they are a gold-star protein choice, are inexpensive and are easy to prepare.

Tip

Butternut squash can be difficult to peel. To make the task easier, first cut the squash in half crosswise, to create two flat surfaces. Place each squash half on its flat surface and use a sharp utility knife to remove the tough peel.

Serving Idea

Serve with a steamed green vegetable such as peas or green beans.

- **Preheat oven to 400°F (200°C)**
- **13- by 9-inch (33 by 23 cm) glass baking dish, lightly greased**

1	butternut squash, peeled and cubed (4 to 5 cups/1 to 1.25 L)	1
1	package (10 oz/300 g) frozen chopped spinach, thawed and drained	1
1½ cups	cubed peeled potatoes	375 mL
¾ cup	thinly sliced red onion	175 mL
8	large eggs	8
½ cup	milk	125 mL
	Freshly ground black pepper	
1 cup	shredded Cheddar cheese	250 mL
½ cup	crumbled feta cheese	125 mL

1. Place squash in a large microwave-safe bowl and cover with plastic wrap, leaving a corner open to vent. Microwave on High for about 5 minutes or until fork-tender. Drain off excess liquid. Gently stir in spinach, potatoes and red onion. Spread in prepared baking dish.

2. In a bowl, whisk together eggs and milk. Season to taste with pepper. Pour over vegetables and stir gently to distribute. Sprinkle evenly with Cheddar and feta.

3. Bake in preheated oven for 35 to 40 minutes or until eggs are set.

This recipe courtesy of dietitian Lindsay Mandryk.

Thai Fish en Papillote

This recipe is a great way to add flavor to fish, which is a good source of iron and omega-3 fats for your baby.

Tips

Mature green mangos have a flavor and texture similar to those of a crisp, tart green apple. Choose one that has an unblemished skin and firm flesh.

Opening the packets at the table makes a dramatic presentation, as guests are enchanted by the aromas.

You can also use frozen fish fillets. Increase the baking time to 15 to 18 minutes.

- **Preheat oven to 425°F (220°C)**
- **4 sheets parchment paper, each about 16 by 12 inches (40 by 30 cm)**

4	pieces skinless salmon fillet or white fish fillets (about 1 lb/500 g total)	4
1 tbsp	grated gingerroot	15 mL
¼ cup	coconut milk	60 mL
2 tsp	fish sauce	10 mL
1 tsp	chile-garlic sauce	5 mL
	Grated zest and juice of 1 lime	
1	red bell pepper, julienned	1
1	green mango (see tip), julienned	1
2 tbsp	fresh cilantro leaves	30 mL
1	lime, cut into 4 wedges	1

1. Place 1 piece of fish on each sheet of parchment paper. Fold all four sides of the paper to form creases about 4 inches (10 cm) from the edge, but do not close. (This will prevent liquids from spilling off the paper.)

2. In a small bowl, combine ginger, coconut milk, fish sauce, chile-garlic sauce, lime zest and lime juice. Drizzle evenly over fish. Divide red pepper and green mango evenly on top of fish. Bring the two long sides of the parchment paper together on top of the fish and fold over repeatedly to close the center, then fold the sides together, tucking the ends under the packet to hold them in place.

3. Place packets on a baking sheet. Bake in preheated oven for 10 to 12 minutes or until fish flakes easily when tested with a fork.

4. Transfer packets to serving plates. Cut paper open with a sharp knife or scissors and add cilantro and a lime wedge to each packet.

This recipe courtesy of dietitian Christina Blais.

Tasty Fish Cakes

Makes 4 servings

My whole family loves these fish cakes. They're a great way to serve salmon, even for those who aren't big fans, as the flavor is mild when mixed with the potatoes.

Tip

Use plain puréed or mashed potato, without milk or butter added.

1	can (7½ oz/213 g) salmon, drained, skin and large bones removed (or 6 oz/175 g leftover cooked salmon)	1
1 cup	puréed or mashed potatoes	250 mL
¼ cup	finely chopped green onion	60 mL
¼ cup	finely chopped red bell pepper	60 mL
3 tbsp	chopped fresh dill	45 mL
3 tbsp	milk	45 mL
	Salt and freshly ground black pepper	
1	large egg, beaten	1
	Nonstick cooking spray	

1. In a medium bowl, combine salmon, potatoes, green onion, red pepper, dill and milk. Season to taste with salt and pepper. Gently stir in egg. Form mixture into four ¾-inch (2 cm) thick cakes. Cover and refrigerate for at least 30 minutes or overnight to let flavor develop.

2. Heat a large nonstick skillet over medium heat. Spray with cooking spray. Add fish cakes and cook for about 2 minutes per side or until browned on both sides and hot in the center.

Variation

Vary the flavor by using 6 oz (175 g) cooked haddock, crab or diced shrimp instead of salmon. Change the herbs and veggies depending on the fish or seafood you choose.

This recipe courtesy of Eileen Campbell.

Salmon Burgers

These salmon burgers are an easy and tasty way to eat salmon, one of the best sources of omega-3 fats, which are important for your baby's brain development.

Tips

For an easy tartar sauce, combine ½ cup (125 mL) mayonnaise with 2 tbsp (30 mL) sweet green pickle relish. Stir to blend.

Garnish with a selection of lettuce, sliced tomato, sliced red onion and sliced red or yellow bell pepper.

1	can (7½ oz/213 g) salmon, drained	1
1	large egg, beaten	1
½ cup	fine dry bread crumbs, divided	125 mL
1 tsp	dried Italian seasoning	5 mL
	Freshly ground black pepper	
2 tbsp	vegetable oil	30 mL
2	onion or whole wheat buns, split and toasted	2
	Tartar sauce (see tip)	

1. In a bowl, combine salmon, egg, ¼ cup (60 mL) bread crumbs, Italian seasoning and pepper to taste. Mix well. Form mixture into 2 patties, about ½ inch (1 cm) thick. Spread the remaining bread crumbs on a plate. Dip each patty into crumbs, covering both sides.

2. In a nonstick skillet, heat oil over medium heat. Add patties and cook, turning once, until hot and golden, about 3 minutes per side.

3. Serve on warm buns slathered with tartar sauce and add your favorite toppings.

Variations

Add ¼ cup (60 mL) finely chopped red or green onion to the salmon.

Add 2 tbsp (30 mL) to ¼ cup (60 mL) finely chopped bell pepper or frozen mixed bell pepper strips, if desired, to the salmon in addition to or instead of the onion. If using frozen mixed pepper strips, remove them from the freezer before you start mixing.

Salmon with Roasted Vegetables

Makes 2 servings

Salmon, sweet potatoes and red peppers are all superfoods — high in nutrients such as omega-3 fats, vitamin C and beta-carotene.

• • • • • • • • • • • • • • • • • • • •

Tip
The tail end of the salmon contains the fewest bones. However, you can substitute two 4-oz (125 g) salmon fillets.

- Preheat oven to 425°F (220°C)
- 11- by 7-inch (28 by 18 cm) baking dish

1 tbsp	olive oil	15 mL
2 tsp	minced garlic	10 mL
2 tsp	dried thyme, divided	10 mL
1 cup	diced peeled sweet potatoes	250 mL
1 cup	diced zucchini or finely chopped red bell peppers	250 mL
1 cup	diced peeled parsnips or potatoes	250 mL
2 tbsp	freshly squeezed lemon juice	30 mL
1/4 tsp	freshly ground black pepper	1 mL
1	salmon tail (8 to 12 oz/250 to 375 g), patted dry	1

1. In a small bowl, stir together olive oil, garlic and 1 tsp (5 mL) thyme. Place sweet potatoes, zucchini and parsnips in baking dish and sprinkle with oil mixture; toss to coat. Spread out vegetables in a single layer and roast in preheated oven for 15 minutes.

2. In the bowl used for oil mixture, combine the remaining thyme, lemon juice and pepper. Brush mixture over salmon tail.

3. Remove vegetables from oven and stir. Place salmon, skin-side down, on top of vegetables. Bake for 10 to 15 minutes or until fish is opaque and flakes easily with a fork. Remove skin from salmon before serving.

Baked "Fried" Chicken

Makes 4 servings

Chicken thighs are a good choice for your baby, as they offer more iron and are more tender than chicken breasts.

Tips

It's very important to line the baking sheet with parchment paper for this dish. Without it, your baking sheet will likely end up with burned spots and the chicken will probably stick.

Be careful not to overcook the chicken or it may become dry.

This method will not work with chicken breasts, as they have insufficient fat and will end up much too dry.

Serving Idea

Serve with mashed sweet potatoes and fresh coleslaw to complete a traditional fried chicken meal.

This recipe courtesy of dietitian Hélène Dufour.

- **Preheat oven to 450°F (230°C)**
- **Large rimmed baking sheet, lined with parchment paper**

½ cup	whole wheat flour	125 mL
3 tbsp	paprika	45 mL
1½ tbsp	dried dillweed	22 mL
1½ tbsp	onion powder	22 mL
½ tsp	celery salt	2 mL
½ tsp	freshly ground black pepper	2 mL
8	boneless skinless chicken thighs	8

1. In a shallow dish, stir together flour, paprika, dill, onion powder, celery salt and pepper.

2. Unfold chicken thighs and dry each piece with a paper towel. Dip each thigh in flour mixture, coating well and shaking off excess coating. Refold thighs loosely and lay on prepared baking sheet. Discard any excess flour mixture.

3. Bake in preheated oven for 30 minutes. Flip each piece over and bake for 20 to 25 minutes or until chicken is crispy and looks fried, juices run clear and a meat thermometer inserted in the thickest part of a thigh registers 165°F (74°C).

Chicken Parmesan Strips

Makes 4 servings

What child doesn't love chicken fingers? This homemade version offers your baby a tasty, easy-to-grasp meat choice. Even if your baby is not a fan of meat, he will likely gobble these up!

• Baking sheet, greased

1 lb	boneless skinless chicken breasts, cut into strips	500 g
½ cup	skim milk	125 mL
⅓ cup	dry bread crumbs or corn flakes cereal, finely crushed	75 mL
3 tbsp	freshly grated Parmesan cheese	45 mL
2 tsp	dried parsley	10 mL
¼ tsp	freshly ground black pepper	1 mL

1. Place chicken in a shallow dish and pour in milk. Cover and refrigerate for at least 15 minutes or for up to 4 hours. Preheat oven to 375°F (190°C).

2. In another shallow dish, combine bread crumbs, Parmesan, parsley and pepper. Remove chicken strips from milk and dip in crumb mixture, coating well. Place on prepared baking sheet. Discard any excess milk and crumb mixture.

3. Bake for 20 minutes or until chicken is no longer pink inside.

Variations
Add other dried herbs, such as thyme, basil or oregano, to the bread crumb mixture.

Replace some of the bread crumbs with ground flax seeds (flaxseed meal).

This recipe courtesy of Patsy Turple.

Pasta with Chicken and Vegetable Sauce

The cooked broccoli in this dish is a great starter veggie for your baby. Not only is broccoli nutrient-dense, but it has a natural handle so it's easy to grasp!

Tips

Cold chicken shredded by hand into irregular, bite-size pieces is more visually appealing and creates more surface area for the flavorful sauce to cling to than cubes cut with a knife.

For the best texture, be careful not to boil the chicken in the sauce.

If your family is just starting to eat whole wheat pasta, mix it half and half with regular pasta at first. Gradually increase the percentage of whole wheat until the whole dish is whole-grain.

This recipe courtesy of dietitian Joanne Rankin.

1 lb	whole wheat penne or rotini pasta	500 g
2 tbsp	canola or olive oil	30 mL
1 cup	chopped onion	250 mL
3	cloves garlic, minced	3
½ tsp	hot pepper flakes (optional)	2 mL
4 cups	bite-size broccoli florets (about 1 large head)	1 L
1 cup	canned no-salt-added diced tomatoes, with juice	250 mL
1½ cups	shredded cooked chicken	375 mL
2 tbsp	basil pesto	30 mL
½ cup	coarsely chopped fresh parsley	125 mL
	Freshly ground black pepper	
½ cup	freshly grated Parmesan cheese	125 mL

1. In a large pot of boiling salted water, cook pasta according to package directions until al dente. Drain, reserving ½ cup (125 mL) of the cooking water. Transfer pasta to a large serving bowl.

2. Meanwhile, in a large skillet, heat oil over medium-high heat. Add onion and cook, stirring, for about 3 minutes or until softened and edges are lightly browned. Add garlic and hot pepper flakes (if using); cook, stirring, for 30 seconds. Add broccoli and cook, stirring occasionally, for about 5 minutes or until bright green.

3. Stir in tomatoes and bring to a boil. Stir in chicken, pesto and reserved pasta water. Reduce heat and simmer, stirring often, for about 3 minutes or until chicken is heated through. Remove from heat and stir in parsley and black pepper to taste.

4. Pour sauce over pasta and stir to combine. Sprinkle with Parmesan.

Variation
Use leftover turkey or meatballs instead of chicken.

Creamy Bow-Ties with Chicken, Spinach and Peppers

Makes 4 servings

This is a delicious meal that your whole family will love. As a bonus, it contains all four food groups in one dish!

• • • • • • • • • • • • • • • • • • • •

Tip

The old Cheddar adds a wonderfully rich flavor to this dish. Other strong-tasting white cheeses, such as Asiago, also work well.

6 oz	bow-tie pasta	175 g
12 oz	boneless skinless chicken breasts, cut into strips	375 g
1 tbsp	vegetable oil, divided	15 mL
1 cup	julienned red bell peppers	250 mL
2 cups	shredded spinach	500 mL
2 tsp	freshly squeezed lemon juice	10 mL
1 tbsp	all-purpose flour	15 mL
1 tsp	minced garlic	5 mL
2 cups	milk	500 mL
¼ tsp	ground nutmeg	1 mL
¼ tsp	freshly ground black pepper	1 mL
¾ cup	shredded sharp (old) white Cheddar cheese	175 mL
¼ cup	freshly grated Parmesan cheese	60 mL

1. In a large pot of boiling water, cook pasta until tender but firm; drain. Rinse under hot water; drain. Transfer to a bowl and set aside.

2. Meanwhile, spray a large skillet with vegetable spray. Add chicken strips and cook over medium-high heat for 4 to 5 minutes or until browned and juices run clear when chicken is pierced with a fork. Transfer to a plate.

3. In the same skillet, heat 1 tsp (5 mL) oil over medium heat. Add peppers and cook, stirring, for 3 to 4 minutes or until slightly softened. Stir in spinach and cook for 1 to 2 minutes or until wilted. Stir in lemon juice. Transfer vegetables to a bowl and set aside.

4. In the same pot used for cooking pasta, heat the remaining oil over medium heat; blend in flour. Add garlic and milk; cook, whisking constantly, until mixture comes to a boil. Reduce heat and simmer for 2 to 3 minutes. Stir in nutmeg and pepper. Remove from heat. Add Cheddar cheese and stir until blended. Add pasta, chicken and vegetables to sauce; stir until combined. Serve sprinkled with Parmesan cheese.

African-Style Braised Chicken in Peanut Sauce

This is a tender, flavorful dish that's good for the whole family. Dark poultry, like the chicken thighs in this recipe, is a good choice for your baby, as it is more tender and higher in iron than chicken breast meat.

Tips

If you prefer, substitute bone-in chicken breasts for the thighs. Leave the skin on and brown them in the oil before softening the vegetables.

This dish can be partially prepared before it is cooked. Complete step 1. Cover and refrigerate for up to 2 days. When you're ready to cook, continue with the recipe.

• **Large (minimum 5-quart) slow cooker**

1 tbsp	vegetable oil	15 mL
2	onions, finely chopped	2
4	cloves garlic, minced	4
1 tsp	dried oregano	5 mL
1/4 tsp	salt	1 mL
1/2 tsp	cracked black peppercorns	2 mL
1/2 cup	ready-to-use low-sodium chicken broth	125 mL
1/2 cup	low-sodium tomato sauce	125 mL
1	bay leaf	1
3 lbs	bone-in skinless chicken thighs (about 12)	1.5 kg
1/2 cup	peanut butter	125 mL
2 tbsp	sherry or freshly squeezed lemon juice	30 mL
2 tsp	curry powder	10 mL
1/2 to 1	long mild red or green chile pepper, minced	1/2 to 1
1	red bell pepper, finely chopped	1
	Hot cooked white rice	

1. In a skillet, heat oil over medium heat for 30 seconds. Add onions and cook, stirring, until softened, about 3 minutes. Add garlic, oregano, salt and peppercorns; cook, stirring, for 1 minute. Stir in broth, tomato sauce and bay leaf; bring to a boil.

2. Arrange chicken over bottom of slow cooker and cover with vegetable mixture. Cover and cook on Low for 6 hours or on High for 3 hours, until juices run clear when chicken is pierced with a fork.

3. In a bowl, combine peanut butter, sherry, curry powder and chile pepper. Add a little cooking liquid and stir to blend. Add to slow cooker along with red bell pepper. Cover and cook on High for 20 minutes, until pepper is tender and flavors meld. Discard bay leaf. Serve over hot white rice.

Simple Chicken Curry

Baby food doesn't have to be bland — babies are allowed spices! Limit salt and added sugar, but a variety of seasonings, like the garam masala and curry in this recipe, will expand your baby's palate.

Tips

Garam masala is a spice blend used in Indian cooking that is available in Asian markets or, increasingly, well-stocked supermarkets.

For the best flavor, toast and grind cumin and fennel seeds yourself. To toast seeds: Place seeds in a dry skillet over medium heat and cook, stirring, until fragrant, about 3 minutes. Immediately transfer to a spice grinder or mortar and grind.

This quantity of cayenne produces a nicely spicy result. If your baby is not a fan, rinse her portion in a colander in the sink.

To make ahead, complete step 1. Cover and refrigerate mixture for up to 2 days. When you're ready to cook, complete the recipe.

• **Medium to large (3½- to 5-quart) slow cooker**

1 tbsp	extra virgin olive oil, virgin coconut oil or ghee	15 mL
2	onions, finely chopped	2
4	cloves garlic, minced	4
1 tbsp	minced gingerroot	15 mL
2 tsp	garam masala (see tip)	10 mL
2 tsp	cumin seeds, toasted and ground (see tip)	10 mL
1 tsp	fennel seeds, toasted and ground	5 mL
1 tsp	cracked black peppercorns	5 mL
1 tsp	ground turmeric	5 mL
1	can (14 oz/398 mL) low-sodium diced tomatoes, with juice	1
1 cup	ready-to-use low-sodium chicken broth	250 mL
2 lbs	skinless bone-in chicken thighs (8 thighs)	1 kg
¼ tsp	cayenne pepper (see tip)	1 mL
1 cup	plain yogurt	250 mL

1. In a skillet, heat oil over medium-high heat. Add onions and cook, stirring, until they begin to turn golden, about 5 minutes. Add garlic, ginger, garam masala, cumin, fennel, peppercorns and turmeric; cook, stirring, for 1 minute. Add tomatoes and broth; bring to a boil.

2. Arrange chicken evenly over bottom of slow cooker and add tomato mixture. Cover and cook on Low for 6 hours or on High for 3 hours, until juices run clear when chicken is pierced with a fork. In a bowl, combine cayenne and yogurt. Stir well. Add to chicken, stir well and cook on Low for 10 minutes to meld flavors.

Light and Easy Chicken Chili

Makes 8 servings

Diced chicken, veggies and beans are great finger foods to pick out and place on your baby-led weaner's tray. If the chili is too spicy, you can rinse it in a colander in the kitchen sink.

Tip
Cut up all the vegetables, measure out all the spices and open up the cans before you start to make the chili; that way, cooking is a snap.

1 tbsp	canola oil	15 mL
2 cups	chopped onions	500 mL
1 cup	chopped carrots	250 mL
1 cup	chopped celery	250 mL
1 cup	chopped red bell pepper	250 mL
2	cloves garlic, minced	2
1 lb	boneless skinless chicken breasts, cut into 1-inch (2.5 cm) cubes	500 g
2 to 3 tbsp	chili powder	30 to 45 mL
2 tsp	ground cumin	10 mL
1 tsp	dried oregano	5 mL
1/4 tsp	hot pepper flakes	1 mL
1	can (19 oz/540 mL) red kidney beans, drained and rinsed	1
1	can (19 oz/540 mL) chickpeas, drained and rinsed	1
1	can (28 oz/796 mL) no-salt-added diced tomatoes, with juice	1
1/4 cup	chopped fresh parsley	60 mL

1. In a large pot, heat oil over medium-high heat. Add onions, carrots, celery and red pepper; cook, stirring, for 4 to 5 minutes or until softened. Add garlic and cook, stirring, for 30 seconds.

2. Add chicken and cook, stirring occasionally, for 7 to 8 minutes or until starting to brown. Add chili powder to taste, cumin, oregano and hot pepper flakes; cook, stirring, for 1 to 2 minutes or until fragrant.

3. Stir in kidney beans, chickpeas and tomatoes; bring to a boil, stirring. Reduce heat and simmer, stirring occasionally, for 30 minutes or until sauce is slightly thickened and chicken is no longer pink inside. Serve garnished with parsley.

This recipe courtesy of Phyllis Quarrie.

Turkey Apple Meatloaf

Meatloaf is a great food for your baby, as it's flavorful, tender and easy to pick up.

- Preheat oven to 350°F (180°C)
- 9- by 5-inch (23 by 12.5 cm) loaf pan, lightly greased

2	cloves garlic, minced	2
1	large egg	1
1	tart apple (such as Mutsu or Granny Smith), finely chopped	1
1 lb	lean ground turkey	500 g
½ cup	chopped onion	125 mL
⅓ cup	oat bran	75 mL
⅓ cup	ground flax seeds (flaxseed meal)	75 mL
3 tbsp	prepared yellow mustard	45 mL
1 tbsp	ketchup	15 mL

1. In a large bowl, combine garlic, egg, apple, turkey, onion, oat bran, flax seeds, mustard and ketchup. Pack into prepared loaf pan.

2. Bake in preheated oven for 45 to 60 minutes or until a meat thermometer inserted in the center registers 165°F (74°C).

Variation

Turkey Apple Burgers: This mixture can also be used to make burgers, which can be cooked on a barbecue or grill or in the oven. They're excellent served on a whole wheat bun with sliced tomato and a spoonful of cucumber dressing.

This recipe courtesy of dietitian Gillian Proctor.

Turkey Sloppy Joes

Makes 6 servings

While you can use any ground meat in this recipe, turkey doesn't just have to be served for Thanksgiving! It's an economical, nutrient-dense meat choice.

Tips

To toast cumin seeds: Place seeds in a dry skillet over medium heat, stirring, until fragrant, about 3 minutes. Immediately transfer to a mortar or a spice grinder and grind. You can substitute 1 tsp (5 mL) ground cumin for the cumin seeds, if you prefer.

This dish can be partially prepared before it is cooked. Complete steps 1 and 2, chilling cooked meat and onion mixtures separately. Cover and refrigerate for up to 2 days. When you're ready to cook, combine and continue with the recipe.

Serving Idea

Serve over hot split onion buns and accompany with a tossed salad for a tasty and nutritious meal.

• **Medium to large (3½- to 6-quart) slow cooker**

2 tbsp	vegetable oil, divided	30 mL
1½ lbs	ground turkey	750 g
2	onions, finely chopped	2
4	cloves garlic, minced	4
2 tsp	cumin seeds, toasted and ground (see tip)	10 mL
2 tsp	dried oregano	10 mL
½ tsp	cracked black peppercorns	2 mL
1 cup	tomato-based chili sauce	250 mL
2 cups	shredded Monterey Jack cheese	500 mL
1	green bell pepper, finely chopped (optional)	1
1	jalapeño pepper, minced (optional)	1
1 tbsp	Worcestershire sauce	15 mL
1 tsp	paprika (preferably smoked)	5 mL
	Hot onion buns	

1. In a skillet, heat 1 tbsp (15 mL) oil over medium heat for 30 seconds. Add turkey and cook, breaking up meat with a wooden spoon, until no longer pink. Using a slotted spoon, transfer to slow cooker. Drain and discard liquid from pan.

2. Add the remaining oil to pan. Add onions and cook, stirring, until softened, about 3 minutes. Add garlic, toasted cumin, oregano and peppercorns; cook, stirring, for 1 minute. Add chili sauce and bring to a boil.

3. Transfer mixture to slow cooker. Cover and cook on Low for 8 hours or on High for 4 hours, until mixture is hot and bubbly. Add cheese, green pepper (if using), jalapeño pepper (if using), Worcestershire sauce and paprika. Cover and cook on High for 20 minutes, until cheese is melted and pepper is softened. Spoon over hot split onion buns and serve.

Super-Moist Turkey Meatballs

Meat is the best-absorbed source of iron, and is high in zinc and vitamin B_{12}. Your baby will love eating these meatballs, as they are tender, tasty and easy to grasp.

Tip

Be very gentle when mixing and forming the meatballs. Overmixing will produce a compact, tough texture.

1	slice whole wheat bread	1
2 tbsp	milk	30 mL
1	large egg, beaten	1
1 lb	lean ground turkey	500 g
¼ cup	chopped fresh parsley	60 mL
3 tbsp	freshly grated Parmesan cheese	45 mL
2 tbsp	roasted garlic (see box), minced	30 mL
2 tbsp	chopped fresh chives	30 mL
2 tbsp	ground flax seeds (flaxseed meal)	30 mL
1 tbsp	chopped fresh rosemary	15 mL
½ tsp	freshly ground black pepper	2 mL
1 tbsp	canola oil	15 mL
⅓ cup	ready-to-use low-sodium chicken broth	75 mL

1. Tear bread into small pieces and place in a large bowl. Cover with milk and let soak for 2 minutes. Add egg, turkey, parsley, cheese, garlic, chives, flax seeds, rosemary and pepper. Using clean hands, gently mix together until evenly incorporated. Form into 1½-tbsp (22 mL) meatballs.

2. In a large nonstick skillet, heat oil over medium-high heat. Add half the meatballs and cook, turning occasionally, for 8 to 10 minutes or until evenly browned on all sides. Transfer to a bowl. Brown the remaining meatballs.

3. Add broth and deglaze the pan, scraping up any brown bits. Return meatballs to the pan, reduce heat to medium-low, cover with a tight-fitting lid and simmer for 5 to 6 minutes or until broth is reduced, leaving minimal liquid, and meatballs are no longer pink inside.

This recipe courtesy of dietitian Kristin Wiens.

Serving Idea

Serve with fresh vegetables and dip, along with a glass of milk, for a delicious lunch for your children.

Variations

Replace the turkey with ground beef, pork or veal, or a mixture of all three meats.

If you prefer a stronger garlic flavor, use 3 cloves minced raw garlic in this recipe.

How to Roast Garlic

Cut off the top of the head, exposing the cloves but not separating them. Place the head on a large square of foil and drizzle with 1 to 2 tsp (5 to 10 mL) oil. Enclose garlic in the foil and roast in a 400°F (200°C) oven for 25 to 30 minutes or until cloves are soft and lightly browned. Let cool. Squeeze garlic cloves out of their papery shells.

White Turkey Chili

Makes 6 servings

This mild, quick chili is a great starter food. Thanks to the turkey and beans, it provides iron and protein in a finger-friendly format.

• • • • • • • • • • • • • • • • • •

Tips

Any other variety of white beans may be used in place of the cannellini beans.

If reduced-sodium salsa verde is not available, use regular salsa verde.

Store the cooled chili in an airtight container in the refrigerator for up to 2 days or in the freezer for up to 6 months. Thaw overnight in the refrigerator or in the microwave using the Defrost function. Warm chili in a medium saucepan over medium-low heat.

1 lb	lean ground turkey	500 g
1 tbsp	ground cumin	15 mL
2 tsp	dried oregano	10 mL
2	cans (each 14 to 19 oz/398 to 540 mL) cannellini (white kidney) beans, drained and rinsed	2
2	jars (each 12 oz/340 mL) mild reduced-sodium salsa verde	2
⅔ cup	water	150 mL
¾ cup	packed fresh cilantro leaves, chopped, divided	175 mL
1 tsp	finely grated lime zest	5 mL
3 tbsp	freshly squeezed lime juice, divided	45 mL
⅔ cup	plain Greek yogurt	150 mL

1. In a large saucepan, cook turkey over medium-high heat, breaking it up with a spoon, for 7 to 10 minutes or until no longer pink. Add cumin and oregano; cook, stirring, for 1 minute.

2. In a small bowl, coarsely mash half the beans with a potato masher or fork. Stir mashed beans, whole beans, salsa and water into the pan. Bring to a boil. Reduce heat to medium-low, cover, leaving lid ajar, and simmer, stirring occasionally, for 10 to 15 minutes or until slightly thickened. Stir in half the cilantro, lime zest and 2 tbsp (30 mL) lime juice. Simmer, uncovered, for 2 minutes.

3. In a small bowl, whisk together yogurt and the remaining lime juice. Serve chili topped with yogurt mixture and the remaining cilantro.

Variation

Substitute lean ground chicken or extra-lean ground pork for the turkey.

Braised Pork with Winter Vegetables

A slow cooker is a busy cook's life-saver! Prep in advance and enjoy super-tender meat that even your baby can eat.

Tip

To make ahead, complete step 2. Cover and refrigerate mixture for up to 2 days. When you're ready to cook, brown the pork and complete the recipe. Or, if you prefer, add the unbrowned pork to the slow cooker along with the vegetable mixture, being aware that the result will not be as flavorful as that produced using browned meat.

- **Large (minimum 5-quart) slow cooker**

2 tbsp	clarified butter or pure lard, divided	30 mL
2 lb	trimmed boneless pork shoulder or blade (butt), patted dry	1 kg
3	onions, thinly sliced on the vertical	3
3	carrots, peeled and diced	3
3	parsnips, peeled and diced	3
6	cloves garlic, minced	6
1 tsp	dried thyme	5 mL
1 tsp	cracked black peppercorns	5 mL
1 cup	ready-to-use low-sodium chicken broth	250 mL
1 tbsp	freshly squeezed lemon juice	15 mL
1	can (28 oz/796 mL) low-sodium tomatoes, with juice, coarsely chopped	1

1. In a large skillet, heat 1 tbsp (15 mL) clarified butter over medium-high heat. Add pork and brown on all sides, about 10 minutes. Transfer to slow cooker.

2. Reduce heat to medium. Add the remaining butter to pan. Add onions, carrots and parsnips; cook, stirring, until softened, about 7 minutes. Add garlic, thyme and peppercorns; cook, stirring, for 1 minute. Add broth and lemon juice; bring to a boil and boil for 2 minutes, scraping up brown bits from bottom of pan. Add tomatoes and return to a boil.

3. Transfer to slow cooker. Cover and cook on Low for 8 hours or on High for 4 hours, until meat is very tender.

Santa Fe–Style Ribs

Ribs are a classic baby-led weaning food. They are a great meat option because rib meat is tender and the bones make the ribs easy to grasp.

Tips

This recipe works best if the ribs are in one big piece when cooked. (This cut is usually only available from a butcher or in the pork roast section of the grocery store.) The single piece is easy to turn while broiling and will basically fall apart into individual servings after the meat is cooked.

This dish can be partially prepared before it is cooked. Complete step 2. Cover and refrigerate for up to 2 days. When you're ready to cook, continue with the recipe.

- **Preheat broiler, with rack set 6 inches (15 cm) from heat source**
- **Large (minimum 5-quart) slow cooker**

3½ to 4 lbs	country-style pork ribs (see tip)	1.75 to 2 kg
2 tbsp	vegetable oil	30 mL
8	cloves garlic, slivered	8
1 tbsp	cumin seeds, toasted and ground (see tip, page 179)	15 mL
1 tsp	dried oregano	5 mL
½ tsp	cracked black peppercorns	2 mL
1	can (28 oz/796 mL) sodium-reduced tomatoes, drained and coarsely chopped	1
2 tbsp	white vinegar	30 mL
	Polenta (optional)	

1. Broil ribs on both sides, until lightly browned, about 7 minutes per side. Drain on paper towels and transfer to slow cooker.

2. In a skillet, heat oil over medium heat for 30 seconds. Add garlic and cook, stirring often, until golden and softened, being careful that the garlic doesn't burn. Add cumin, oregano and peppercorns; cook, stirring, for 1 minute. Stir in tomatoes and vinegar and bring to a boil.

3. Pour sauce over ribs. Cover and cook on Low for 6 hours or on High for 3 hours, until ribs are tender and falling off the bone. Cut pork into individual ribs if a whole piece of meat was used and place on a deep platter. (If desired, spread a layer of polenta on platter first.) Cover with sauce and serve.

Classic Beef Stew

Makes 6 servings		

Beef stew is one of the best starter dishes for your baby, as it's full of soft veggies and iron-rich beef. The whole family will love this comfort food dish!

- **Medium to large (3½- to 5-quart) slow cooker**

1 tbsp	vegetable oil	15 mL
2 lbs	stewing beef, cut into 1-inch (2.5 cm) cubes and patted dry	1 kg
2	onions, finely chopped	2
4	stalks celery, thinly sliced	4
2	large carrots, peeled and diced	2
2	cloves garlic, minced	2
1 tsp	dried thyme	5 mL
¼ tsp	salt	1 mL
½ tsp	cracked black peppercorns	2 mL
2	bay leaves	2
¼ cup	all-purpose flour	60 mL
2 cups	ready-to-use low-sodium beef broth	500 mL
½ cup	water	125 mL
	Finely chopped fresh parsley leaves	

1. In a skillet, heat oil over medium-high heat. Add beef, in batches, and brown, about 4 minutes per batch. Using a slotted spoon, transfer to slow cooker.

2. Reduce heat to medium. Add onions, celery and carrots; cook, stirring, until vegetables are softened, about 7 minutes. Add garlic, thyme, salt, peppercorns and bay leaves; cook, stirring, for 1 minute. Add flour and cook, stirring, for 1 minute. Add broth and water; cook, stirring, until thickened.

3. Transfer to slow cooker and stir well. Cover and cook on Low for 8 hours or on High for 4 hours, until beef is very tender. Discard bay leaves. Just before serving, garnish liberally with parsley.

Variation

Beef Stew with Roasted Garlic: Mash 6 cloves roasted garlic and stir into stew before garnishing with parsley. An easy way to roast this quantity of garlic is to peel the cloves, remove the pith (the center part that often sprouts) then place the cloves on a piece of foil. Drizzle about ½ tsp (2 mL) olive oil over the garlic, then fold up the foil to make a tight packet. Bake in a 400°F (200°C) oven for 20 minutes.

Beef Pot Pie

If you like slow-cooking roasts for your baby, this recipe is good for using up the extras. And who doesn't love a pot pie?

Tips

You can use leftover cooked potatoes and carrots instead of cooking them in step 1.

Clean mushrooms with a damp cloth. Do not immerse them in water — they soak it up like a sponge. Store fresh mushrooms in the refrigerator for up to 1 week in a paper bag, rather than in plastic, where they are too moist and become slimy.

This recipe courtesy of Sharon Deters Dusyk.

- **Preheat oven to 450°F (230°C)**
- **12-cup (3 L) casserole dish, lightly greased**

2 cups	cubed peeled potatoes (1/2-inch/1 cm cubes)	500 mL
1 cup	cubed carrots (1/2-inch/1 cm cubes)	250 mL
3 tbsp	butter, non-hydrogenated margarine or canola oil	45 mL
1 cup	sliced mushrooms	250 mL
1/2 cup	chopped onion	125 mL
2	cloves garlic, minced	2
1/3 cup	all-purpose flour	75 mL
1/2 tsp	freshly ground black pepper	2 mL
2 cups	ready-to-use low-sodium beef broth	500 mL
3/4 cup	milk	175 mL
1 tsp	fresh thyme leaves	5 mL
2 cups	cubed leftover cooked roast beef (1/2- to 3/4-inch/1 to 2 cm cubes)	500 mL
1/2 cup	frozen green peas	125 mL

Biscuit Topping

1 1/2 cups	all-purpose flour	375 mL
2 tsp	baking powder	10 mL
1/2 tsp	salt	2 mL
1/3 cup	cold butter or non-hydrogenated margarine	75 mL
1 tbsp	finely snipped fresh chives (optional)	15 mL
3/4 cup	milk	175 mL

1. Place potatoes and carrots in a pot and add enough cold water to cover. Bring to a boil over medium-high heat; reduce heat and simmer for 6 to 8 minutes or until vegetables are fork-tender. Drain and set aside.

2. Meanwhile, in a large nonstick skillet, melt butter over medium-high heat. Add mushrooms and onion; cook, stirring, for 3 to 4 minutes or until onion is softened. Add garlic and cook, stirring, for 30 seconds. Stir in flour and pepper; cook, stirring, for 1 minute.

Tip

Add only warm or cool liquid to a roux (a fat and flour mixture). If you add cold liquid, the fat in the roux could become more solid, creating lumps that are difficult to dissolve.

3. Gradually stir in broth, milk and thyme; bring to a boil, stirring often. Reduce heat and simmer, stirring occasionally, for 3 to 4 minutes or until sauce is thickened.

4. Stir in cooked potatoes and carrots, beef and peas; bring to a boil. Reduce heat and simmer, stirring often, for about 5 minutes or until heated through. Pour into prepared casserole dish.

5. *Topping:* In a large bowl, combine flour, baking powder and salt. Using a pastry blender or two knives, cut in butter until mixture resembles coarse crumbs. Stir in chives (if using). Add milk and stir with a fork until just combined. Drop 12 biscuits on top of beef mixture.

6. Bake in preheated oven for 20 minutes or until biscuits are golden and sauce is bubbling.

Variation

Use sweet potatoes instead of white potatoes, and frozen corn instead of peas.

Beef Noodle Casserole

The slow cooker is a great tool for making family-friendly meals. The ingredients in this dish come out so tender, they're easy for even a toothless baby to eat!

Tip

This dish can be partially prepared before it is cooked. Complete steps 1 and 2, chilling cooked meat and onion mixture separately. Refrigerate for up to 2 days. When you're ready to cook, continue cooking as directed in the recipe. If the tomato mixture has thickened with chilling, heat it gently until it is a spreadable consistency. To facilitate preparation, the night before you plan to cook this casserole, shred Cheddar cheese, cover and refrigerate.

• **Large (minimum 5-quart) oval slow cooker, lightly greased**

2 tbsp	vegetable oil, divided	30 mL
1 lb	lean ground beef	500 g
2	onions, finely chopped	2
4	stalks celery, thinly sliced	4
4	cloves garlic, minced	4
2 tsp	dried oregano	10 mL
1 tsp	cracked black peppercorns	5 mL
1 cup	ready-to-use low-sodium beef broth	250 mL
1 cup	low-sodium tomato sauce	250 mL
4 oz	cream cheese, softened and cubed	125 g
8 oz	egg noodles, cooked and drained	250 g

Cheddar Crumb Topping

1 cup	dry bread crumbs	250 mL
2 tbsp	melted butter	30 mL
1 cup	shredded Cheddar cheese	250 mL

1. In a skillet, heat 1 tbsp (15 mL) oil over medium-high heat for 30 seconds. Add beef and cook, stirring and breaking up with the back of a spoon, until no longer pink, about 5 minutes. Remove with a slotted spoon and set aside. Drain off liquid in pan.

2. Reduce heat to medium and add the remaining oil to pan. Add onions and celery; cook, stirring, until softened, about 5 minutes. Add garlic, oregano and peppercorns; cook, stirring, for 1 minute. Add broth, tomato sauce and cream cheese; cook, stirring, until cheese is melted.

3. Spoon $1/2$ cup (125 mL) tomato sauce mixture into bottom of slow cooker. Cover with half of the meat, then half of the noodles. Repeat layers of meat and noodles. Finish with a layer of sauce. Cover and cook on Low for 5 to 6 hours or on High for $2^1/2$ to 3 hours, until mixture is hot and bubbly.

4. *Topping:* In a bowl, combine bread crumbs and butter. Add cheese and stir well. Spread over casserole and cook on High for 30 minutes, until cheese is melted and top is bubbly.

Veggie, Beef and Pasta Bake

This is a perfect family-friendly casserole. You can't go wrong with pasta, veggies, beef and cheese — yum!

Tip

This recipe is delicious served sprinkled with hot pepper flakes or hot pepper sauce, for the adults in the family who prefer a little kick.

Nutrition Tip

One tbsp (15 mL) regular soy sauce contains 1,037 mg sodium; the same amount of sodium-reduced, or light, soy sauce contains about 605 mg.

- **Preheat oven to 350°F (180°C)**
- **13- by 9-inch (33 by 23 cm) baking dish, greased**

1 lb	lean ground beef	500 g
1 cup	sliced onions	250 mL
1 cup	diced zucchini	250 mL
2 tsp	minced garlic	10 mL
1	can (28 oz/796 mL) no-salt added stewed or diced tomatoes, with juice	1
2 tbsp	sodium-reduced soy sauce	30 mL
2 cups	rotini (or other spiral pasta)	500 mL
1½ cups	shredded Cheddar cheese	375 mL

1. In a large nonstick skillet over medium-high heat, combine ground beef, onions, zucchini and garlic; cook, stirring, for 8 to 10 minutes or until beef is no longer pink and vegetables are softened. Drain fat; pour beef mixture into baking dish. Set aside.

2. Meanwhile, drain juice from tomatoes into an 8-cup (2 L) microwave-safe measuring cup; add water to make 2 cups (500 mL). Roughly chop tomatoes and add to measuring cup. Stir in soy sauce. Microwave on High for 5 minutes or until very hot. Stir in rotini.

3. Pour tomato-pasta mixture into baking dish and combine with meat mixture. Press pasta down to make sure it is submerged in the liquid. Bake in preheated oven, covered, for 20 minutes. Remove cover, stir gently and sprinkle with cheese. Bake, uncovered, for 15 to 20 minutes or until pasta is tender.

This recipe courtesy of Kathryn Papple.

Spaghetti Sauce

Serve this pasta sauce with rotini, which is easy for your baby to grasp. Freeze any extras for a quick meal on busy nights.

Nutrition Tip

Making your own spaghetti sauce allows you to keep the sodium content low, compared to store-bought options.

12 oz	lean ground beef	375 g
1	small onion, chopped	1
1	clove garlic, minced	1
1	can (19 oz/540 mL) stewed low-sodium tomatoes, with juice, chopped	1
1	can (5½ oz/156 mL) tomato paste	1
¼ cup	chopped green bell pepper	60 mL
1 tbsp	dried basil	15 mL
½ tsp	crushed fennel seeds	2 mL
Pinch	freshly ground black pepper	Pinch

1. In a large skillet over medium heat, brown ground beef, breaking up chunks. Add onion, garlic, tomatoes, tomato paste, green pepper, basil, fennel seeds and pepper; bring to a boil. Reduce heat and simmer, stirring occasionally, for 20 to 30 minutes or until vegetables are tender and flavor is well developed.

Variation
Substitute ground bison for the beef, if you like. Bison is even higher in iron than beef!

This recipe courtesy of dietitian Judy Jenkins.

Snacks

Roasted Red Pepper and Feta Hummus

Makes about 2 cups (500 mL)

This mixture of chickpeas and red peppers provides a great combination of non-heme iron and vitamin C for your baby's growth. Hummus is a great dip for breadsticks or veggies, or spread for toast or sandwiches.

Tips

Tahini is a paste or butter made from crushed sesame seeds. It has a distinctive nutty taste and coarse texture. It is frequently used in Middle Eastern cooking.

You can also use an immersion blender to process the ingredients.

Serving Idea

Serve with pita or an assortment of fresh vegetables.

- Food processor or blender

2	red bell peppers, roasted and peeled (see box)	2
2	cloves garlic, minced	2
1	can (19 oz/540 mL) chickpeas, drained and rinsed	1
½ cup	crumbled feta cheese	125 mL
2 tbsp	chopped fresh parsley	30 mL
2 tbsp	tahini	30 mL
2 tbsp	freshly squeezed lemon juice	30 mL
2 tbsp	water	30 mL
1 tbsp	canola oil	15 mL
¼ tsp	cayenne pepper	1 mL
½	lemon	½

1. In food processor, combine roasted peppers, garlic, chickpeas, feta, parsley, tahini, 2 tbsp (30 mL) lemon juice, water, oil and cayenne; process until smooth.

2. Transfer to a bowl, cover and refrigerate for at least 1 hour, until chilled, or for up to 1 day. Squeeze fresh lemon juice over dip before serving.

Variation

Substitute unsweetened natural peanut butter for the tahini.

How to Roast Red Peppers

To roast your own red peppers, quarter peppers and remove seeds. Place skin side up on a rimmed baking sheet in a 450°F (230°C) oven and roast for 10 minutes. Turn peppers over and roast for 10 to 15 minutes or until skins are blackened. Transfer peppers to a small bowl, cover tightly and let stand for about 15 minutes. When cool enough to handle, peel off blackened skin and discard.

This recipe courtesy of dietitian Trisha Wood.

Kids' Favorite Fondue

Makes 6 servings

This cheese and tomato fondue is fun for the whole family. Even babies will be able to dip a breadstick or veggie strip into the fondue and lick it off.

Tips

Give everyone their own fondue fork and serve with thick slices of French baguette, quartered, celery sticks or slices of green pepper.

If you're in a hurry, bring the tomatoes to a boil on top of the stove after they have been processed. Then transfer to the slow cooker. Reduce the cooking time in step 1.

- **Small (maximum 3½-quart) slow cooker**
- **Blender or food processor**
- **Fondue forks**

1	can (28 oz/796 mL) low-sodium tomatoes, with juice	1
1 tsp	dried oregano	5 mL
	Freshly ground black pepper	
3 cups	shredded Cheddar cheese	750 mL
	Sliced baguette	
	Celery sticks	
	Sliced green bell pepper	

1. In blender, process tomatoes until relatively smooth. Transfer to slow cooker. Add oregano and pepper to taste; cook on High for 1 hour, until tomatoes are bubbly.

2. Add cheese to slow cooker in handfuls, stirring to combine after each addition. Reduce heat to Low and serve, or cover and keep on Low until ready to serve. Using fondue forks, dip bread or vegetables into fondue.

This recipe courtesy of Marilyn Linton.

Sardine and Pesto Spread

Sardines are one of the best sources of the omega-3 fat DHA. Even if you turn up your nose at canned sardines, your baby may surprise you and love them!

Tips

Don't mash the sardines too much, or you'll end up with more of a paste than a spread.

Try Mediterranean-style or lemon-flavored sardines.

1	can (3½ oz/106 g) sardines, drained	1
2 tbsp	basil pesto	30 mL
1 tbsp	freshly squeezed lime juice	15 mL

1. In a small bowl, mash sardines with a fork. Stir in pesto and lime juice until just blended.

Nutrition Tip
Sardines are a good choice for people trying to increase their intake of vitamin B_{12} and iron.

Serving Idea
Serve with crudités, whole-grain crackers or toasted French baguette slices.

This recipe courtesy of dietitian Claude Gamache.

Crispy Kale Chips

These crunchy chips are easier for little ones to eat than sautéed or raw kale. Kale is high in vitamins C, A and K, as well as many other antioxidants.

- Preheat oven to 325°F (160°C)
- 2 rimmed baking sheets, lined with parchment paper

1 lb	kale, rinsed and patted dry	500 g
	Nonstick cooking spray (preferably olive oil)	
¼ tsp	salt	1 mL

1. Remove tough stems and center ribs from kale, then tear leaves into approximately 3-inch (7.5 cm) pieces. Arrange leaves in a single layer on prepared baking sheets. Spray with cooking spray and sprinkle with salt.

2. Bake in preheated oven for 12 to 15 minutes or until edges are browned and leaves are crispy. Serve warm or let cool completely on pans.

Baked Masala Puri

Makes 25 puri

I started making homemade crackers for my baby when he was plowing through baby rice crackers in 3 seconds flat! These are more flavorful and nutritious, and are great served with hummus (see page 192) to dip.

Tips

Puri (often spelled "poori") are unleavened breads of Indian origin. They are traditionally large breads that are fried and then filled with curries; here, they are made into small, cracker-type morsels and baked.

For an evenly browned color on the puri, place the baking sheet on the middle rack of the oven and bake one sheet at a time.

Serving Idea

These puri are great on their own as a snack, but also make great entertaining fare when paired with a dip or spread.

This recipe courtesy of dietitian Shefali Raja.

- **Preheat oven to 325°F (160°C)**

½ cup	whole wheat flour	250 mL
1 tbsp	canola oil	15 mL
2 tsp	sesame seeds	10 mL
½ tsp	ground cumin	2 mL
½ tsp	freshly ground black pepper	2 mL
¼ tsp	ground turmeric	1 mL
¼ tsp	salt	1 mL
¼ cup	chopped fresh cilantro (optional)	60 mL
2 tbsp	water (approx.)	30 mL

1. In a medium bowl, combine whole wheat flour, oil, sesame seeds, cumin, pepper, turmeric, salt and cilantro (if using). Add a small amount of water and mix with your hands to form a stiff dough.

2. Turn dough out onto a floured surface and knead for 2 to 3 minutes or until dough is soft and smooth. Leave dough on floured surface and cover with large bowl. Let rest for 10 minutes.

3. Divide dough into 25 equal portions. On a lightly floured surface, roll out each portion into a thin round, about 2 inches (5 cm) in diameter. Prick with a fork and place at least 2 inches (5 cm) apart on baking sheets.

4. Bake in preheated oven for 15 minutes. Flip puri over and bake for 10 minutes or until golden brown. Remove from oven and let cool.

Variation

If a stronger sesame taste is desired, use 1½ tsp (7 mL) each sesame oil and canola oil.

Quick Whole Wheat Breadsticks

Makes 18 breadsticks

Breadsticks make a great first dipping tool, before your baby is ready to use utensils. Serve with a thick soup that your baby can dip them into.

Tip

Store breadsticks in an airtight container in the refrigerator for up to 3 days.

- Preheat oven to 375°F (190°C)
- Food processor
- Large rimmed baking sheet, lined with parchment paper

2 cups	whole wheat pastry flour	500 mL
¾ tsp	salt	3 mL
½ tsp	baking powder	2 mL
3 tbsp	cold unsalted butter or virgin coconut oil	45 mL
⅔ cup	ice water	150 mL
	Nonstick cooking spray (preferably olive oil)	

1. In food processor, pulse flour, salt and baking powder to combine. Add butter and pulse until mixture resembles fresh, moist bread crumbs. With the motor running, through the feed tube, add ice water and process just until dough comes together.

2. Transfer dough to a lightly floured work surface and pat into a 1-inch (2.5 cm) thick rectangle. Roll out to a 12- by 10-inch (30 by 25 cm) rectangle about ¼ inch (0.5 cm) thick. Using a sharp knife or pizza cutter, cut dough crosswise into ¼-inch (0.5 cm) thick strips.

3. Gently roll each strip into a 14-inch (35 cm) long stick. Brush 1 stick with water and twist it with another stick, pressing at the top and the bottom. Repeat with the remaining sticks. Arrange twists at least 1 inch (2.5 cm) apart on prepared baking sheet. Spray twists lightly with cooking spray.

4. Bake in preheated oven for 20 to 25 minutes or until golden brown. Let cool in pan on a wire rack for 5 minutes, then transfer to the rack to cool.

Sweet Potato Muffins

These muffins make an easy on-the-go snack and are far more nutritious than store-bought muffins, thanks to the addition of sweet potato, dried fruit, wheat germ and whole wheat flour.

Tip

For the mixed dried fruit, try raisins, blueberries, cherries and cranberries.

- **Preheat oven to 400°F (200°C)**
- **12-cup muffin tin, lightly greased or lined with paper cups**

1 cup	quick-cooking rolled oats	250 mL
1 cup	buttermilk (approx.)	250 mL
½ cup	all-purpose flour	125 mL
½ cup	whole wheat flour	125 mL
¼ cup	granulated sugar	60 mL
1 tbsp	wheat germ	15 mL
1 tbsp	baking powder	15 mL
½ tsp	salt	2 mL
½ tsp	baking soda	2 mL
1 cup	mixed dried fruit, chopped	250 mL
1	large egg, beaten	1
½ cup	grated sweet potato	125 mL
¼ cup	lightly packed brown sugar	60 mL
¼ cup	vegetable oil	60 mL
1 tsp	grated orange zest	5 mL

1. Place oats in a large bowl and pour in buttermilk; stir to combine. Cover and let stand for 10 minutes.

2. Meanwhile, in a small bowl, combine all-purpose flour, whole wheat flour, granulated sugar, wheat germ, baking powder, salt and baking soda. Stir in dried fruit.

3. In another small bowl, combine egg, sweet potato, brown sugar, oil and orange zest. Stir into oats mixture. Gradually fold in flour mixture until just moistened. If too stiff, add a little more buttermilk.

4. Divide batter evenly among prepared muffin cups, filling almost to the top (these muffins do not rise much).

5. Bake for 20 minutes or until a tester inserted in the center of a muffin comes out clean. Let cool in tin for 10 minutes, then transfer to a wire rack to cool completely.

This recipe courtesy of Eileen Campbell.

Date Bars

Dates serve as the perfect natural, nutritious sweetener for these bars. They also function as the "glue," which is why they are included in so many homemade bar recipes.

Tips

For the best results, use whole pitted dates and chop them yourself. Pre-chopped dates are typically tossed with oat flour (to prevent sticking) and sugar. In addition, they tend to be fairly hard. If pre-chopped dates are the only option available, give them a quick rinse in hot (not boiling) water to remove any coatings and soften them slightly.

Store the cooled bars in an airtight container in the refrigerator for up to 5 days.

- Preheat oven to 375°F (190°C)
- Blender or food processor
- 8-inch (20 cm) square metal baking pan, sprayed with nonstick cooking spray

1¼ cups	quick-cooking rolled oats	300 mL
½ cup	whole wheat flour	125 mL
½ tsp	ground cardamom or cinnamon	2 mL
½ tsp	baking powder	2 mL
¼ tsp	salt	1 mL
⅔ cup	chopped pitted dates, divided	150 mL
1 tsp	finely grated orange zest	5 mL
¼ cup	freshly squeezed orange juice	60 mL
¼ cup	vegetable oil	60 mL
1	large egg, at room temperature	1

1. In a medium bowl, whisk together oats, flour, cardamom, baking powder and salt.

2. In blender, combine half the dates, orange zest, orange juice and oil; purée until very smooth. Add egg and blend until just combined.

3. Add the date mixture to the oats mixture, stirring until just blended. Gently fold in the remaining dates.

4. Spread batter evenly in prepared pan.

5. Bake in preheated oven for 15 to 20 minutes or until golden brown and set at the center. Let cool completely in pan on a wire rack. Cut into 16 bars.

Fruit and Nut Raw Energy Bars

Makes 6 bars

These bars have a texture similar to a soft fruit leather, with nuts added. Pecans are high in healthy monounsaturated fat, and are fine to add to your baby's diet once she is 6 months old.

Tips

Place a square of plastic wrap or waxed paper on top of the sticky fruit-nut mixture to help press it into the prepared pan.

You can also roll the fruit-nut mixture into 1-inch (2.5 cm) balls instead of making bars.

Store bars in an airtight container at room temperature for up to 1 week or in the refrigerator for up to 3 weeks. Or wrap them in plastic wrap, then foil, completely enclosing them, and freeze for up to 6 months. Let thaw at room temperature for 1 hour before serving.

- **Food processor**
- **9- by 5-inch (23 by 12.5 cm) metal loaf pan, lined with foil (see tip, page 200), foil sprayed with nonstick cooking spray**

¾ cup	packed pitted Medjool dates	175 mL
¾ cup	dried cranberries or dried cherries	175 mL
1 cup	pecan halves	250 mL
¼ tsp	ground cinnamon	1 mL

1. In food processor, pulse dates and cranberries until mixture resembles a thick paste. Transfer to a medium bowl.

2. In the same food processor (no need to clean it), pulse pecans until finely chopped. Add pecans and cinnamon to fruit paste and, using your fingers or a wooden spoon, combine well.

3. Firmly press mixture into prepared pan. Refrigerate for 15 minutes. Using foil liner, lift mixture from pan and invert onto a cutting board. Peel off foil and cut into 6 bars.

Variations

Apricot Almond Energy Bars: Reduce the dates to ½ cup (125 mL) and replace the cranberries with 1 cup (250 mL) packed soft dried apricots. Substitute almonds for the pecans and omit the cinnamon.

PB&J Energy Bars: Replace the pecans with raw peanuts and omit the cinnamon.

Cashew "Cookie Dough" Energy Bars: Increase the dates to 1 cup (250 mL) and omit the cranberries. Substitute 1½ cups (375 mL) cashews for the pecans and omit the cinnamon.

Chocolate Chip "Cookie Dough" Energy Bars: Increase the dates to 1 cup (250 mL) and omit the cranberries. Substitute 1½ cups (375 mL) cashews for the pecans. Add 2 oz (60 g) very finely chopped semisweet or bittersweet (dark) chocolate and 1 tsp (5 mL) vanilla extract. Decrease the cinnamon to ⅛ tsp (0.5 mL).

Pistachio Energy Bars: Increase the dates to 1 cup (250 mL) and omit the cranberries. Substitute 1½ cups (375 mL) pistachios for the pecans, add ¼ tsp (1 mL) almond extract and omit the cinnamon.

Toasted Quinoa Energy Bars

You can add snacks like these delicious bars in addition to meals once your baby is between 9 and 12 months old.

Tips

Lining a pan with foil is easy. Begin by turning the pan upside down. Tear off a piece of foil longer than the pan, then mold the foil over the pan. Remove the foil and set it aside. Flip the pan over and gently fit the shaped foil into the pan, allowing the foil to hang over the sides (the overhang ends will work as "handles" when the contents of the pan are removed).

You can also form the quinoa mixture into 1-inch (2.5 cm) balls instead of making bars.

Store bars in an airtight container at room temperature for up to 1 week or in the refrigerator for up to 3 weeks. Or wrap them in plastic wrap, then foil, completely enclosing them, and freeze for up to 6 months. Let thaw at room temperature for 1 hour before serving.

- Food processor
- 8- by 4-inch (20 by 10 cm) metal loaf pan, lined with foil (see tip) and sprayed with nonstick cooking spray

1 cup	quinoa, rinsed	250 mL
¾ cup	packed pitted Medjool dates	175 mL
¾ cup	dried cranberries or dried cherries	175 mL
¼ tsp	ground cinnamon	1 mL

1. Heat a large skillet over medium-high heat. Toast quinoa, stirring occasionally, for 3 to 4 minutes or until golden brown and just beginning to pop. Transfer to a large bowl and let cool.

2. In food processor, pulse dates and cranberries until mixture resembles a thick paste. Transfer to a medium bowl.

3. In the same food processor (no need to clean it), pulse cooled quinoa 3 to 4 times or until roughly chopped. Add to fruit paste, along with cinnamon. Using your fingers or a wooden spoon, combine well.

4. Using your hands, a spatula or a large piece of waxed paper, press quinoa mixture firmly into prepared pan. Refrigerate for 15 minutes. Using foil liner, lift mixture from pan and invert onto a cutting board. Peel off foil and cut into 6 bars.

Variation

Apricot Energy Bars: Reduce the dates to ½ cup (125 mL) and replace the cranberries with 1 cup (250 mL) packed soft dried apricots.

Quinoa Cashew Power Balls

Makes 16 balls

Dark molasses contains iron and also serves as a natural sweetener in this recipe.

Tips

Look for roasted cashews lightly seasoned with sea salt.

Store cooled power balls in an airtight container at room temperature for up to 3 days. Or wrap them in plastic wrap, then foil, completely enclosing them, and freeze for up to 6 months. Let thaw at room temperature for 2 to 3 hours before serving.

- Baking sheet
- Food processor
- Rimmed baking sheet, lined with parchment paper

⅔ cup	quinoa, rinsed	150 mL
1⅓ cups	water	325 mL
1½ cups	lightly salted roasted cashews	375 mL
1 tsp	ground cinnamon	5 mL
1½ tbsp	dark (cooking) molasses	22 mL
1½ tbsp	pure maple syrup	22 mL
1 tsp	vanilla extract	5 mL

1. In a large saucepan, combine quinoa and water. Bring to a boil over medium-high heat. Reduce heat to low, cover and simmer for 14 to 16 minutes or until water is absorbed. Fluff with a fork. Spread quinoa on unlined baking sheet and refrigerate until completely cooled.

2. Preheat oven to 375°F (190°C).

3. In food processor, pulse cashews until finely chopped. Add cooled quinoa, cinnamon, molasses, maple syrup and vanilla; pulse until mixture forms a dough.

4. Roll dough into 16 balls of equal size. Place on prepared baking sheet.

5. Bake in preheated oven for about 20 minutes or until golden brown. Let cool in pan on a wire rack for 10 minutes, then transfer to the rack to cool.

Zucchini Quinoa Fritters

Your baby will love the taste of these soft, nutritious fritters. Let her practice dipping the fritters in yogurt.

Tip

You can find quinoa flour in the health food section of your grocery store or make your own (see box, page 124).

1 lb	zucchini (about 2 medium), coarsely shredded	500 g
1 tsp	salt	5 mL
1	large egg	1
½ cup	packed fresh basil leaves, chopped	125 mL
½ cup	quinoa flour	125 mL
¼ tsp	freshly cracked black pepper	1 mL
	Olive oil	
½ cup	plain Greek yogurt	125 mL

1. Place zucchini in a colander set in the sink and sprinkle with salt. Let drain for 10 minutes, then press out as much liquid as possible.

2. In a large bowl, whisk egg. Stir in zucchini, basil, quinoa flour and pepper until blended.

3. In a large nonstick skillet, heat 2 tsp (10 mL) oil over medium heat. For each fritter, drop about ¼ cup (60 mL) batter into skillet and flatten slightly. Cook for 2 to 3 minutes per side or until browned. Transfer to a plate lined with paper towels. Repeat with the remaining batter, adding more oil and adjusting heat as necessary between batches. Serve immediately, with yogurt.

Quinoa Popovers

Makes 6 popovers

These popovers are a much easier way for your baby to eat quinoa than if you serve it as a plain side dish. They're great alongside a slow-cooked roast and steamed veggies, or on their own as a snack.

Tips

You can find quinoa flour in the health food section of your grocery store or make your own (see box, page 124).

No matter how tempting the aroma coming from your oven as they bake, resist opening the oven to check them until about 5 minutes before they're finished baking; check too soon, and they will deflate.

These popovers may also be made in a 12-cup muffin pan with 6 cups buttered. Reduce the second baking time by about 5 minutes.

If using a 12-cup popover pan or muffin pan, butter every other cup for even baking.

- **Preheat oven to 450°F (230°C)**
- **Blender or food processor**
- **6-cup nonstick popover pan, generously buttered**

1 cup	quinoa flour	250 mL
¼ tsp	salt	1 mL
3	large eggs, at room temperature	3
1 cup	milk	250 mL
1 tbsp	unsalted butter, melted, or olive oil	15 mL

1. In blender, combine flour, salt, eggs, milk and butter; process until smooth.

2. Divide batter equally among prepared popover cups.

3. Bake in preheated oven for 10 minutes. Without opening oven door, reduce heat to 375°F (190°C). Bake for 15 to 20 minutes or until puffed and golden brown. Run a thin knife between the edge of each popover and the cup to loosen. Lift popovers from cups and serve immediately.

Variations

Sharp Cheddar Quinoa Popovers: Add 1 tsp (5 mL) Dijon mustard and a pinch of cayenne pepper in step 1. Sprinkle popovers with ½ cup (125 mL) shredded extra-sharp (extra-old) Cheddar cheese before the final 5 minutes of baking.

Parmesan Sage Quinoa Popovers: Add ¼ cup (60 mL) freshly grated Parmesan cheese and 1 tsp (5 mL) dried sage in step 1. Sprinkle popovers with an additional ¼ cup (60 mL) Parmesan before the final 5 minutes of baking.

...t Wrap

Makes 1 serving

This quick snack combines three food groups, and could also make a good breakfast option.

¼ cup	yogurt (any flavor)	60 mL
1	10-inch (25 cm) whole wheat tortilla	1
3	strawberries, sliced	3
½	small banana, sliced	½
2 tbsp	granola (optional)	30 mL

1. Spread yogurt up the middle of the tortilla. Place strawberry slices, banana slices and granola (if using) on top of the yogurt. Roll up tortilla.

Variation
You can substitute ricotta cheese, cream cheese or cottage cheese for the yogurt.

This recipe courtesy of dietitian Lisa Zappotelli.

Pita Surprise

Makes 1 serving

A mini pita makes the perfect little pocket, easy for little hands to hold without the fillings falling out! They can be a bit tougher for younger weaners to chew, but in that case they will have fun picking out and eating the cheese and apple.

¼	apple, chopped (with or without peel)	¼
	Ground cinnamon	
1	mini whole wheat pita	1
1 tsp	shredded Cheddar cheese	5 mL

1. Sprinkle chopped apple with enough cinnamon to coat evenly.

2. Cut an opening in the top of the pita. Spoon apple pieces into pita. Spoon cheese on top of apples.

Variations
Swap in chopped pear for the apple.

Use any cheese you have on hand.

This recipe courtesy of dietitian Patricia Wright.

Desserts

Mango Mousse

Mangos are a delicious source of vitamin C and fiber. Who knew dessert could be tasty and nutrient-dense at the same time?

This recipe courtesy of dietitian Claude Gamache.

- Food processor

1	bag (20 oz/600 g) frozen mango chunks, thawed and drained	1
½ cup	vanilla-flavored yogurt	125 mL
1 cup	sliced strawberries	250 mL
1 cup	blueberries	250 mL

1. In food processor, purée mango and yogurt for 1 minute or until smooth.

2. Divide mousse among serving bowls. Top with strawberries and blueberries and serve immediately, or cover and refrigerate for up to 12 hours, then top with berries before serving.

Five-Minute Cheesecake Cups with Raspberries

Makes 2 servings

This is a healthy dessert, providing plenty of protein, thanks to the cottage cheese! Along with the raspberries, it produces a delicious sweet-salty taste combo.

- Food processor
- Two 6-oz (175 mL) ramekins or dessert glasses

1 cup	cottage cheese	250 mL
1 tbsp	pure maple syrup	15 mL
½ tsp	vanilla extract	2 mL
⅔ cup	raspberries	150 mL
2 tbsp	finely chopped lightly salted roasted pistachios	30 mL

1. In food processor, combine cottage cheese, maple syrup and vanilla; purée until smooth.

2. Divide mixture between ramekins. Top with raspberries and pistachios.

Pumpkin Pie Tarts with Ground Almond Crust

This recipe
courtesy of dietitian
Judy Campbell-Gordon.

Makes 8 servings

Using ground nuts as a crust gives these healthy individual pumpkin pies extra nutrients, without sacrificing taste!

Tip
You can make these tarts up to 2 days before you plan to serve them. Cover each ramekin with plastic wrap and refrigerate. Remove from refrigerator 30 minutes before serving.

- **Preheat oven to 400°F (200°C)**
- **Eight ½-cup (125 mL) heatproof ramekins, greased**
- **2 baking sheets**

½ cup	ground almonds	125 mL
2	large eggs, beaten	2
1¼ cups	canned pumpkin purée (not pie filling)	300 mL
½ cup	sweetened condensed milk	125 mL
1 tsp	ground cinnamon	5 mL
½ tsp	ground ginger	2 mL
¼ tsp	ground cloves	1 mL
¼ tsp	ground nutmeg	1 mL

1. Place 4 ramekins on each baking sheet. Divide ground almonds among prepared ramekins.

2. In a medium bowl, whisk together eggs, pumpkin, milk, cinnamon, ginger, cloves and nutmeg until well blended. Divide evenly among ramekins.

3. Bake in preheated oven for 10 minutes. Reduce oven temperature to 350°F (180°C) and bake for 12 to 15 minutes or until mostly set (the middle of the tarts should still jiggle slightly). Let cool completely in ramekins on a wire rack.

Variation
Use ground pecans instead of almonds.

Blackberry Peach Cobbler

Makes 6 servings

The sugar in this recipe comes from the sweet fruit. Choose nice ripe peaches — nature's candy!

Tip

You can substitute 2 cans (each 14 oz/398 mL) sliced peaches, drained, for the fresh and use an equal quantity of frozen blackberries, thawed.

- **Small (maximum 3½-quart) slow cooker, lightly greased**

4	peaches, peeled and sliced	4
3 cups	blackberries	750 mL
1 tbsp	freshly squeezed lemon juice	15 mL
1 tbsp	cornstarch	15 mL

Topping

1½ cups	all-purpose flour	375 mL
2 tsp	baking powder	10 mL
½ tsp	salt	2 mL
1 tsp	grated lemon zest	5 mL
½ cup	cold butter, cut into 1-inch (2.5 cm) cubes	125 mL
½ cup	milk	125 mL

1. In prepared slow cooker, combine peaches, blackberries, lemon juice and cornstarch. Stir well. Cover and cook on Low for 4 hours or on High for 2 hours.

2. *Topping:* In a bowl, combine flour, baking powder, salt and lemon zest. Using your fingers or a pastry blender, cut in butter until mixture resembles coarse crumbs. Drizzle with milk and stir with a fork until a batter forms.

3. Drop batter by spoonfuls over hot fruit. Cover and cook on High for 1 hour, until a tester inserted in the center comes out clean.

No-Bake Raspberry Thumbprints

Makes 36 cookies

These soft cookies are perfect for little hands. The dates, nut butter and coconut create a tasty treat that is far more nutritious than the store-bought variety.

Tips

You can use any unsweetened natural nut or seed butter, such as peanut butter, cashew butter or sunflower butter, in place of the almond butter.

There's no need to clean the food processor bowl between steps 2 and 3.

Store these cookies in the fridge, or they get quite gooey.

- Food processor
- Large baking sheet, lined with parchment paper

¾ cup	chopped pitted dates	175 mL
	Hot water	
3 cups	large-flake (old-fashioned) rolled oats	750 mL
½ cup	unsweetened flaked coconut	125 mL
½ tsp	ground cinnamon	2 mL
¼ tsp	salt	1 mL
1 tsp	finely grated orange zest	5 mL
¼ cup	freshly squeezed orange juice	60 mL
1½ cups	unsweetened natural almond butter	375 mL
⅓ cup	raspberry or other fruit jam sweetened with fruit juice	75 mL

1. Place dates in a medium bowl and add enough hot water to cover. Let soak for 15 minutes. Drain, reserving ½ cup (125 mL) soaking liquid.

2. Meanwhile, in food processor, combine oats, coconut, cinnamon and salt; pulse until coarsely ground. Transfer to a large bowl.

3. In food processor, combine soaked dates, the reserved soaking liquid, orange zest and orange juice; purée until smooth.

4. Add the date mixture and almond butter to the oat mixture, mixing with a wooden spoon or your hands to make a cohesive dough.

5. Roll dough into thirty-six 1-inch (2.5 cm) balls. Place on prepared baking sheet. Using your thumb, make a small indentation in the center of each ball. Loosely cover with foil or plastic wrap and refrigerate for at least 1 hour, until chilled, or store in an airtight container in the refrigerator for up to 1 week. Just before serving, spoon ¼ tsp (1 mL) jam into each indentation.

Fruit Pyrohy

Makes 35 to 40 pyrohy

Filled with fruit and dusted with cinnamon sugar, this unique dessert is sure to become a family favorite!

Tips

For the fruit, try any combination of berries, plums and/or cherries.

If you use frozen fruit, do not thaw it. Sweeten it slightly, if desired, and toss with up to ½ cup (125 mL) all-purpose flour to keep the juices from running out as the fruit thaws.

The pyrohy dough can be left out, covered, for several hours. It becomes softer with resting.

Variation

Instead of the fruit filling, try using a purchased poppy seed filling.

This recipe courtesy of dietitian Dianna Bihun.

Dough

3 cups	all-purpose flour (approx.)	750 mL
Pinch	salt	Pinch
1 tbsp	canola oil	15 mL
1½ cups	warm water	375 mL

Fruit Filling

4 cups	finely chopped fresh seasonal fruit (see tips)	1 L
	Granulated sugar (optional)	

Topping

2 tbsp	granulated sugar	30 mL
1 tsp	ground cinnamon	5 mL

1. *Dough:* In a large bowl, combine flour and salt. Gradually add oil, then warm water, incorporating flour with a wooden spoon as you pour. Stir until mixture holds together. Transfer to a lightly floured work surface and knead for about 10 minutes, until a soft and pliable dough forms, adding more flour as necessary to prevent sticking. Invert the bowl over the dough and let rest for at least 10 minutes.

2. *Filling:* In a bowl, combine fruit and sugar to taste (if using).

3. Pinch off a ball of dough about the diameter of a golf ball. On a clean, lightly floured surface, roll out the dough until it is very thin (no thicker than about ⅛ inch/3 mm) and 2 to 2½ inches (5 to 6 cm) in diameter. Place the circle in the palm of your hand and place about 1 tsp (5 mL) filling in the center. Fold the circle in half and press the edges together with your fingers, making sure no filling has seeped through to the edges. Place pyrohy on a lightly floured board or work surface and cover with a clean tea towel. Do not let them stick together. Repeat with the remaining dough and filling.

4. In a large pot of boiling water, boil 10 to 15 pyrohy at a time, stirring gently with a wooden spoon to separate and prevent sticking, for 3 to 5 minutes or until puffed. Using a slotted spoon, transfer pyrohy to a serving dish.

5. *Topping:* In a small bowl, combine sugar and cinnamon. Sprinkle over pyrohy.

Coconut Pudding

While this recipe is a bit sweeter thanks to the condensed milk, it's okay to offer your older baby. Homemade desserts can also contain some good nutrients, such as the eggs and coconut here.

Tips

To toast coconut, preheat oven to 300°F (150°C). Spread coconut in a thin, even layer on an ungreased baking sheet. Bake for 15 to 20 minutes, stirring every 5 minutes, until golden brown and fragrant. Transfer to a plate and let cool completely.

It can be beneficial to offer your baby the odd sweet, so that sweets are not a coveted or forbidden food as your child grows older — just make sure not to use sweets as a reward for eating dinner!

- **Large (minimum 5-quart) oval slow cooker**
- **4-cup (1 L) lightly greased baking dish**

1	can (14 oz/398 mL) coconut milk	1
1 tbsp	grated lime zest	15 mL
1 tbsp	minced gingerroot	15 mL
1 cup	sweetened condensed milk	250 mL
3	large eggs, beaten	3
½ cup	unsweetened shredded coconut, toasted (see tip)	125 mL

1. In a saucepan over medium heat, combine coconut milk, lime zest and ginger. Bring just to a boil. Remove from heat and stir in condensed milk. Let cool. Whisk in eggs. Strain through a fine sieve into prepared dish. Fold in coconut.

2. Cover with foil and secure with string. Place dish in slow cooker and pour in enough boiling water to come 1 inch (2.5 cm) up the outside of the dish. Cover and cook on High for 2½ to 3 hours, until a tester inserted in the center of the pudding comes out clean. Serve warm or chilled.

Toasted Coconut Banana Quinoa Pudding

Makes 6 servings

This mild, tasty dessert is also packed with nutrition! Coconut milk is high in lauric acid, which is a type of saturated fat also found in high levels in breast milk.

• **Blender or food processor**

1 cup	quinoa, rinsed	250 mL
2 cups	water	500 mL
2 cups	coconut milk	500 mL
1 cup	mashed ripe bananas	250 mL
3 tbsp	pure maple syrup	45 mL
1/2 tsp	ground ginger	2 mL
1/8 tsp	salt	0.5 mL
2 tsp	vanilla extract	10 mL
1/2 cup	unsweetened flaked coconut, toasted (see tip, page 211)	125 mL

1. In a medium saucepan, combine quinoa and water. Bring to a boil over medium-high heat. Reduce heat to low, cover and simmer for 12 to 15 minutes or until liquid is absorbed.

2. Meanwhile, in blender, combine coconut milk, bananas, maple syrup, ginger and salt; purée until smooth.

3. Stir banana mixture into quinoa and cook over medium heat, stirring constantly, for 10 to 12 minutes or until thickened. Remove from heat and stir in vanilla.

4. Transfer quinoa mixture to a medium heatproof bowl and let cool to room temperature. Serve at room temperature or cover and refrigerate until cold. Serve sprinkled with toasted coconut.

Chocolate Pudding

If you're opposed to a huge mess, offer your baby a dipping utensil if she's not quite yet ready for a spoon. Or get the camera ready!

Tip

If a 15-oz (425 mL) can of pumpkin isn't available, purchase a 28-oz (796 mL) can and measure out 1¾ cups (425 mL). Refrigerate extra pumpkin in an airtight container for up to 1 week.

- **Blender or food processor**
- **Six 6-oz (175 mL) ramekins or dessert glasses**

1 cup	chopped pitted dates	250 mL
¾ cup	raw cashews	175 mL
	Very hot water	
1	can (15 oz/425 mL) pumpkin purée (not pie filling)	1
¾ cup	coconut milk	175 mL
½ cup	unsweetened cocoa powder	125 mL
1 tsp	vanilla extract	5 mL
	Raspberries (optional)	

1. Place dates and cashews in a medium bowl and add enough very hot water to cover. Let soak for 1 hour to soften. Drain well.

2. In blender, combine date mixture, pumpkin and coconut milk; purée for 1 to 2 minutes or until very smooth. Add cocoa and vanilla; process for 1 minute or until well blended.

3. Divide mixture among ramekins. Cover and refrigerate for at least 1 hour, until chilled, or for up to 1 day. Garnish with raspberries, if desired.

Chocolate Surprise Pudding Pops

Makes 4 large pops

Banana and avocado produce a smooth texture and add nutrients to these pudding pops.

This recipe courtesy of Donna Suerich.

- Blender
- Large ice pop molds

1	large avocado, peeled and pitted	1
1	very ripe banana	1
½ cup	milk	125 mL
2 tbsp	unsweetened cocoa powder	30 mL
1 tsp	vanilla extract	5 mL

1. In blender, on high speed, blend avocado, banana, milk, cocoa and vanilla until smooth.

2. Pour into molds and insert sticks. Freeze until firm, about 6 hours or overnight.

Frozen Tropical Vacation Pops

Makes 12 servings

Ice pops are a nice relief for babies who are teething. The frozen fruit and yogurt will help to calm swollen gums.

Tips

There is no need to use a blender; in fact, it's better to make this by hand, as chunks of banana add to the texture.

Be sure to choose 100% unsweetened juice, not just in this recipe but always!

This recipe courtesy of Kelly Hajnik.

- Frozen pop molds or paper cups with sticks

2	ripe bananas, mashed	2
1 cup	coconut-flavored yogurt	250 mL
1 cup	unsweetened orange juice	250 mL

1. In a bowl, combine bananas, yogurt and juice until well blended.

2. Pour banana mixture into molds and insert sticks. Freeze for at least 4 hours, until solid, or for up to 5 days.

Variation

Vary the juice and yogurt to your liking, but always use the banana for the best texture.

Pink Strawberry Wiggles

Makes 16 servings

Who didn't love Jell-O Jigglers as a child? These are a fun and more nutritious variation of the classic.

Tip

For fun, let kids choose a cookie cutter to make their own shapes.

This recipe courtesy of Marion French.

- **8-inch (2 L) square baking pan**

3 cups	pink or red fruit juice (such as grapefruit or cranberry-raspberry)	750 mL
4	envelopes (each ¼ oz/7 g) unflavored gelatin	4
1 tbsp	cold water	15 mL
1 cup	strawberry-flavored yogurt (or raspberry-flavored)	250 mL

1. In a medium saucepan, heat juice to boiling.

2. In a large, heatproof bowl, whisk together gelatin and cold water. Gradually whisk in boiling juice until gelatin is dissolved. Gradually add yogurt, whisking until well combined. Pour into pan, cover and refrigerate until firm, about 3 hours. Cut into squares and serve.

Cocoa Truffles

Makes 2 dozen truffles

Packed with dates and nuts, these chocolatey truffles make a nutritious dessert or easy-to-go snack — or can provide the cure for Mom's chocolate craving!

Tip

Store the truffles in an airtight container in the refrigerator for up to 1 week.

- **Food processor**

2 cups	pecan halves	500 mL
	Cold water	
2 cups	packed chopped pitted dates	500 mL
⅔ cup	unsweetened cocoa powder	150 mL
¼ tsp	salt	1 mL
1 tbsp	vanilla extract	15 mL

1. Place pecans in a medium bowl and add enough cold water to cover. Let soak for 4 to 6 hours to soften. Drain well.

2. In food processor, pulse softened pecans until chopped. Add dates, cocoa, salt and vanilla; process until almost smooth, stopping once or twice to scrape sides of bowl.

3. Transfer pecan mixture to a medium bowl. Cover and refrigerate for at least 2 hours or until firm enough to roll.

4. Roll pecan mixture into 1-inch (2.5 cm) balls.

Cocoa, Quinoa and Cashew Truffles

....

Makes 2 dozen truffles

Dates are high in fiber and serve as a natural sweetener in this recipe. Combined with cocoa, they create truffles with a nice, rich chocolatey flavor.

. . . .

Tips

Either Dutch process or natural cocoa powder may be used in this recipe, but natural cocoa powder is preferred for its deep, true chocolate flavor and minimal processing.

Store the truffles in an airtight container in the refrigerator for up to 1 week.

• **Food processor**

1 cup	raw cashews	250 mL
	Cold water	
1 cup	cooked quinoa, cooled	250 mL
2 cups	packed chopped pitted dates	500 mL
⅔ cup	unsweetened cocoa powder	150 mL
¼ tsp	salt	1 mL
1 tbsp	vanilla extract	15 mL
	Additional unsweetened cocoa powder (optional)	

1. Place cashews in a medium bowl and add enough cold water to cover. Let soak for 4 to 6 hours to soften. Drain well.

2. In food processor, pulse softened cashews and quinoa until mixture becomes a paste. Add dates, cocoa, salt and vanilla; process until almost smooth, stopping once or twice to scrape sides of bowl. Transfer to a medium bowl, cover and refrigerate for at least 2 hours or until firm enough to roll.

3. Roll quinoa mixture into 1-inch (2.5 cm) balls. If desired, roll in cocoa to coat.

Contributing Authors

Dietitians of Canada
Cook!
Recipes from this book are found on pages 118, 122–23, 134, 136–38, 143, 144 (bottom), 147–48, 150–52, 154–56, 162, 164–68, 171, 173, 177, 180, 186, 192, 194 (top), 195, 206 (top), 207, 210 and 214 (bottom).

Dietitians of Canada
Great Food Fast
Recipes from this book are found on pages 121, 153, 170, 174 and 189.

Dietitians of Canada
Simply Great Food
Recipes from this book are found on pages 116 (top), 120 (bottom), 135, 158–59, 172, 178, 190, 197, 204, 214 (top) and 215 (top).

Judith Finlayson
150 Best Slow Cooker Recipes
Recipes from this book are found on pages 185 and 193.

Judith Finlayson
The 163 Best Paleo Slow Cooker Recipes
Recipes from this book are found on pages 176 and 183.

Judith Finlayson
175 Essential Slow Cooker Classics
Recipes from this book are found on pages 145, 161, 163, 175, 179, 184, 188, 208 and 211.

Judith Finlayson
The Complete Whole Grains Cookbook
A recipe from this book is found on page 117.

Judith Finlayson
The Convenience Cook
Recipes from this book are found on pages 160 and 169.

Jennifer House
Recipes by this author, written for this book, are found on pages 94–108 and 110–113.

Camilla V. Saulsbury
5 Easy Steps to Healthy Cooking
Recipes from this book are found on pages 109, 116 (bottom), 119, 120 (top), 127, 129, 131–132, 139, 140–42, 144 (top), 146, 182, 194 (bottom), 196, 198–99, 201, 206 (bottom), 209, 213 and 215 (bottom).

Camilla V. Saulsbury
500 Best Quinoa Recipes
Recipes from this book are found on pages 124–26, 128, 130, 149, 200, 202–3, 212 and 216.

References

Andersson O, Hellström-Westas L, Andersson D, Domellöf M. (2011, November 15). Effect of delayed versus early umbilical cord clamping on neonatal outcomes and iron status at 4 months: A randomised controlled trial. *BMJ*; 343: d7157.

Bisgaard H, Stokholm J, Chawes BL, et al. (2016, December 29). Fish oil-derived fatty acids in pregnancy and wheeze and asthma in offspring. *N Engl J Med*; 375 (26): 2530–39.

Brown A, Lee M. (2011, January). A descriptive study investigating the use and nature of baby-led weaning in a UK sample of mothers. *Matern Child Nutr*; 7 (1): 34–47.

Brown A, Lee MD. (2015, February). Early influences on child satiety-responsiveness: The role of weaning style. *Pediatr Obes*; 10 (1): 57–66.

Cameron SL, Heath AL, Taylor RW. (2012, November 2). How feasible is Baby-led Weaning as an approach to infant feeding? A review of the evidence. *Nutrients*; 4 (11): 1575–1609.

Cameron SL, Heath AL, Taylor RW. (2012, November 26). Healthcare professionals' and mothers' knowledge of, attitudes to and experiences with, Baby-Led Weaning: A content analysis study. *BMJ Open*; 2 (6): e001542.

Cameron SL, Taylor RW, Heath AL. (2013, December 9). Parent-led or baby-led? Associations between complementary feeding practices and health-related behaviours in a survey of New Zealand Families. *BMJ Open*; 3 (12): e003946.

Cameron SL, Taylor RW, Heath AL. (2015, August 26). Development and pilot testing of Baby-Led Introduction to SolidS — a version of Baby-Led Weaning modified to address concerns about iron deficiency, growth faltering and choking. *BMC Pediatr*; 15: 99.

Centers for Disease Control and Prevention. (2016, December 19). Raw milk questions and answers. Retrieved from www.cdc.gov/foodsafety/rawmilk/raw-milk-questions-and-answers.html.

Collings R, Harvey LJ, Hooper L, et al. (2013, July). The absorption of iron from whole diets: A systematic review. *Am J Clin Nutr*; 98 (1): 65–81.

Du Toit G, Roberts G, Sayre PH, et al. (2015, February 26). Randomized trial of peanut consumption in infants at risk for peanut allergy. *N Engl J Med*; 372 (9): 803–13.

Eneli IU, Crum PA, Tylka TL. (2008, October). The trust model: A different feeding paradigm for managing childhood obesity. *Obesity* (Silver Spring); 16 (10): 2197–204.

Fangupo LJ, Heath AM, Williams SM, et al. (2016, October). A baby-led approach to eating solids and risk of choking. *Pediatrics*; 138 (4): e20160772.

Fulkerson JA, Story M, Mellin A, et al. (2006, September). Family dinner meal frequency and adolescent development: Relationships with developmental assets and high-risk behaviors. *J Adolesc Health*; 39 (3): 337–45.

Gillard BK, Simbala JA, Goodglick L. (1983, June). Reference intervals for amylase isoenzymes in serum and plasma of infants and children. *Clin Chem*; 29 (6): 1119–23.

Hammons AJ, Fiese BH. (2011, June). Is frequency of shared family meals related to the nutritional health of children and adolescents? *Pediatrics*; 127 (6): 1565–74.

Heitlinger LA, Lee PC, Dillon WP, Lebenthal E. (1983, January). Mammary amylase: A possible alternate pathway of carbohydrate digestion in infancy. *Pediatr Res*; 17 (1): 15–18.

Institute of Medicine. (2001). Food and Nutrition Board. *Dietary Reference Intakes for Vitamin A, Vitamin K, Arsenic, Boron, Chromium, Copper, Iodine, Iron, Manganese, Molybdenum, Nickel, Silicon, Vanadium, and Zinc: A Report of the Panel on Micronutrients.* Washington, DC: National Academy Press. Retrieved from: www.nap.edu/read/10026/chapter/1.

Lee PC, Werlin S, Trost B, Struve M. (2004, August). Glucoamylase activity in infants and children: Normal values and relationship to symptoms and histological findings. *J Pediatr Gastroenterol Nutr*; 39 (2): 161–65.

Lindberg T, Skude G. (1982, August). Amylase in human milk. *Pediatrics*; 70 (2): 235–38.

Mangels AR, Messina V. (2001, June). Considerations in planning vegan diets: Infants. *J Am Diet Assoc*; 101 (6): 670–77.

Melina V, Craig W, Levin S. (2016, December). Position of the Academy of Nutrition and Dietetics: Vegetarian diets. *J Acad Nutr Diet*; 116 (12): 1970–80.

Morison BJ, Taylor RW, Haszard JJ, et al. (2016, May 6). How different are baby-led weaning and conventional complementary feeding? A cross-sectional study of infants aged 6–8 months. *BMJ Open*; 6 (5): e010665.

Morzel M, Palicki O, Chabanet C, et al. (2011, July). Saliva electrophoretic protein profiles in infants: Changes with age and impact of teeth eruption and diet transition. *Arch Oral Biol*; 56 (7): 634–42.

O'Donnell MD, Miller NJ. (1980, July 1). Plasma pancreatic and salivary-type amylase and immunoreactive trypsin concentrations: Variations with age and reference ranges for children. *Clin Chim Acta*; 104 (3): 265–73.

Ogunshe AAO, Lahan DA, David OJ, Verissimo OP. (2013). Parental perceptions and microbial/public health implications of pre-chewed weaning foods. *Food Pub Health*; 3 (6): 315–22.

Olsen SF, Secher NJ, Tabor A, et al. (2000, March). Randomised clinical trials of fish oil supplementation in high risk pregnancies. Fish Oil Trials in Pregnancy (FOTIP) Team. *BJOG*; 107 (3): 382–95.

Rowan H, Harris C. Baby-led weaning and the family diet. A pilot study. (2012, June). *Appetite*; 58 (3): 1046–49.

Satter EM. (1996, September). Internal regulation and the evolution of normal growth as the basis for prevention of obesity in children. *J Am Diet Assoc*; 96 (9): 860–64.

Satter E. (2007, September–October). Eating competence: Definition and evidence for the Satter Eating Competence model. *J Nutr Educ Behav*; 39 (5 Suppl): S142–53.

Sevenhuysen GP, Holodinsky C, Dawes C. (1984, April). Development of salivary alpha-amylase in infants from birth to 5 months. *Am J Clin Nutr*; 39 (4): 584–88.

Stephen A, Alles M, de Graaf C, et al. (2012, July). The role and requirements of digestible dietary carbohydrates in infants and toddlers. *Eur J Clin Nutr*; 66 (7): 765–79.

Szajewska H, Shamir R, Mearin L, et al. (2016, March). Gluten introduction and the risk of coeliac disease: A position paper by the European Society for Pediatric Gastroenterology, Hepatology, and Nutrition. *J Pediatr Gastroenterol Nutr*; 62 (3): 507–13.

Townsend E, Pitchford NJ. (2012, February 6). Baby knows best? The impact of weaning style on food preferences and body mass index in early childhood in a case-controlled sample. *BMJ Open*; 2 (1): e000298.

Wright CM, Cameron K, Tsiaka M, Parkinson KN. (2011, January). Is baby-led weaning feasible? When do babies first reach out for and eat finger foods? *Matern Child Nutr*; 7 (1): 27–33.

Zlotkin SH, Ste-Marie M, Kopelman H, et al. (1996, May). The prevalence of iron depletion and iron-deficiency anaemia in a randomly selected group of infants from four Canadian cities. *Nutr Res*; 16 (5): 729–33.

Zoppi G, Andreotti G, Pajno-Ferrara F, et al. (1972, December). Exocrine pancreas function in premature and full term neonates. *Pediatr Res*; 6 (12): 880–86.

Resources

Further Information

Ellen Satter Institute
Information on the division of responsibility in feeding
www.ellynsatterinstitute.org

EWG's Consumer Guide to Seafood
Information on low-mercury fish choices
www.ewg.org/research/ewg-s-consumer-guide-seafood/mercury-toxicity

First Step Nutrition
Nutrition information and advice from Jennifer House
www.firststepnutrition.com

Solid Steps to Babyled Weaning
Baby-led weaning e-course by Jennifer House
www.solidstepstoblw.com

Recommended Products

Doidy Cup
Slanted training cups
www.doidycup.com or www.doidycup.ca

Lucky Iron Fish
A product you add to cooking water to add iron to your dishes
www.luckyironfish.com

Munchkin 360
Spoutless cups and other baby gear
www.munchkin.com

NumNum GOOtensils
Dipper spoons for babies learning to use a spoon
www.numnumbaby.us

Wean Green
Eco-friendly tempered glass food storage containers
www.weangreen.com

Library and Archives Canada Cataloguing in Publication

House, Jennifer, 1980-, author
    The parents' guide to baby-led weaning : with 125 recipes / Jennifer House, MSc, RD.

Includes index.
ISBN 978-0-7788-0579-3 (softcover)

    1. Baby foods. 2. Infants — Nutrition. 3. Infants — Weaning. 4. Cookbooks. I. Title.

RJ216.H68 2017   641.3'00832   C2017-902741-7

Index